# Kennebec

## *Cradle of Americans*

by

Robert P. Tristram Coffin

Down East Books
Camden, Maine

Cover painting © 2002 by Trevor Paul Roberson

ISBN 0-89272-554-0

Down East Books
www.nbnbooks.com

Originally published as part of the Rivers of America series
by Holt, Rinehart and Winston.

# Kennebec

To my son,
Richard

Who has the pilgrim basket,
the Merrymeeting farm,
and who will grow up,
I know,
into a Merrymeeting kind of man.

CHART of the KENNEBEC River Maine

# Contents

# Preface

## The Cradle of the Kennebec

There is probably no more eloquent piece of furniture than a cradle. An empty one, especially. It means a great deal to families. I have a small son who carries around with him as his favorite plaything the pilgrim basket he slept in coming across the Atlantic when he was two months old. He cannot be separated from it. He knows the story and the cradle means a lot to him.

In case there are folks who do not know, a Maine pilgrim basket is a stout capacious vessel woven of straw, with a tight-fitting lid. The name has come down with the pattern, no doubt, from the old Canterbury model, which held a pilgrim's lunch and all his earthly goods by day on the holy march and cradled his baby through the night at the inn or in the starlit fields.

Most rivers are empty cradles today. They once were important parts of the earth. They were bright wedges driven into the New World forests. And the first Americans cut their teeth on their rocks and were sung to sleep by their white music. They cradled the first towns. The rhythm of their flow was built into their children's hearts. They were the first highways. But today, railroads and motor roads have cut across them and sucked their life away. The people now move against the grain of rivers. But rivers did their work for our country and did it well.

The Kennebec is such a cradle. It was one of the first breeders of American men. It rocked pioneers for many of the future states farther west. It rocked the men who were hunters, fishermen, farmers, sailors, and lumbermen all in one, who went west to settle the states of New York, Ohio, Michigan, Wisconsin, Minnesota, Washington, and Oregon. It taught Americans how to make the most of wild game and fish, the soil, the water, and lumber. And its children were some of the stoutest America has had all through her history. No wonder, for they were toughened young. The farms of New York State and Ohio and Minnesota were opened, many of them, by men from Maine. When the forests of Michigan and Wisconsin and Oregon were cut, men who had learned lumbering along the Kennebec and the Penobscot were there to do it. When the trees of Oregon and Washington were built into ships and went out from Puget Sound over the Pacific, the sons of Maine's sea-captain families were on hand to build them and steer them. The history of Maine is this. Maine sent her best to lay the foundations of other states. It has always been so. And the Kennebec has been one of the best of all Maine cradles of manhood.

# 1 The River

The Kennebec is, as Maine people would put it, quite a river. It begins at Moosehead, Maine's largest lake, runs due south 150 miles through the heart of Maine, picks up the Androscoggin, sired by the White Mountains, at Merrymeeting, goes on out through the fine lacework of coast islands, and empties into the Atlantic. It follows the line of Maine's geologic foundation. It drains the greater part of the state. It has hundreds of lakes in its system. It flows through forests and farmlands. Its water-power facilities—if you reckon in the tributary Androscoggin—are probably unsurpassed in the world. It has a score of fine harbors on its lower reaches. George Weymouth, the early explorer, said that the whole Royal Navy could ride in one of them. And so it could, even the Royal Navy of today. It used to be the best fishing grounds of any in North America. It could be so again.

But these are common things, bread-and-butter things, and other American rivers can claim some of them.

The Kennebec has more to it than fine water power and harbors. It has a history that no other stream can match. The dragon-headed Viking ships probably nosed up it. It was a fishing station for many a European nation in the sixteenth century. Even the Spaniards of St. Augustine very likely dried hake and haddock here. The first settlements of the English in the New World were at its mouth. The first ship built in the Western Hemisphere by Englishmen was built here. It was followed by other ships, until almost every farmhouse had an annex that touched on coasts on the other side of the sea. The Kennebec fed the colonists at Plymouth with its corn and fish when the wolf

howled at the Pilgrims' doors. It had flourishing villages
when the rest of New England was still a savage wilderness.
It fed Europe with sturgeon and other fine fish, it sent
beaver skins for the tall hats of Europe's grandees. Church
of Englanders, juicy and more robust men than those of
Massachusetts Bay, came to its banks to live fat and breed
handsome. Other races came early too: Morovian Germans, Huguenot French, Dutch from New Amsterdam.
One of the stoutest of American Colonials, Sir William
Phips, a sea captain who sailed his way to a title and had a
finger in all the more important Colonial pies, was born
and bred in the Kennebec region and left his name on a
Kennebec town. The bloodiest and most savage of the
Indian wars sent up screams and smoke from scores of
Kennebec towns.

The drama played along this river helped largely to de-
termine whether the French or the Anglo-Saxon civilization should control the continent. Stout Kennebec men
helped to crack the hardest link in the French chain of
fortresses strung across North America—Louisburg. Later
on, the Revolution came home to the people of the valley,
since many of the inhabitants were Royalists. The most
spectacular expedition in American history followed the
river up to Quebec, when Arnold tried to do with a handful of Americans what great Wolfe had accomplished only
by means of the flower of the whole British army. An
Indian princess who puts Pocahontas into the shade flourished on Swan Island in the Kennebec and probably com-
plicated the lives of Aaron Burr, Benedict Arnold, and
other men of the Quebec expedition. And in the next war,
an epic naval battle was fought at Kennebec's mouth, when
the *Enterprise* beat the *Boxer* and both captains died in
their lace on the decks. There is a story that Talleyrand fell
into its brook at Hallowell and a house at Edgecomb was
furnished and kept ready for the Queen of France, Marie
Antoinette.

Twelve years after entering the union, a Kennebec
city—Augusta—became its capital; and its first governor,
who had walked barefoot to the Kennebec to make his fortune, driving his yoke of steers ahead of him, was found for

the state, living like a nabob among his fine French furniture at Bath. Nabobs came to be a common thing in that town on the Kennebec. For, in the nineteenth century, Maine took the lead and held it in the building of sailing vessels. The Kennebec turned out ships that tied the river's destiny to all the ports of Christendom and heathendom. Almost every farm had its ship, anchored or making, at the foot of the corn patch. From a dozen flourishing hamlets—Richmond, Hallowell, Woolwich, Bowdoinham, and Phippburg—farmers went to sea, looked forward to shopping days in Batavia and Singapore, to honeymoons that brushed on Cape Horn, and came back and set up housekeeping with the best furniture from the four corners of the earth.

The river stood first in the eighteenth- and nineteenth-century history of lumbering. Logs for half the world came shooting down its rapids. Paul Bunyan took his American name and set his ax to his first tall trees here. Then, in the latter years of the nineteenth century, the Kennebec ice became famous half the world over.

But these, too, are glories that time can dim. There are other more lasting triumphs for the Kennebec River. One of the oldest and best of the American colleges sprang up on its Androscoggin arm. And an American classic that helped to bring on the Civil War, *Uncle Tom's Cabin*, was written in the shadow of that college. Bowdoin's Longfellow and Hawthorne drank of the springs that flow into Kennebec's Merrymeeting Bay, and so on into the sea. Longfellow's *Hesperus* was built at Hallowell. Ward went out into the world from the Kennebec region and taught Americans how to laugh. One of the three greatest American poets, Edwin Arlington Robinson, was brought up in Gardiner, on the Kennebec, and learned to know human nature by knowing the men of the cities and farms of the valley.

My river has everything a person could ask of a river. Great events and greater men. And that nothing of sweetness should be lacking, an old-time fiddler went and fell off a steamer below Bath and left his name on the maps in Fiddler's Reach.

Along the Kennebec, quiet now and no longer
whitened by high sails, dozens of lovely little towns sleep
the sleep of serenity. Fine white mansions under elms and
white churches that immortalize the name of Wren point
up above blue bays and islands of sheer evergreen laces.
They once had roots deep over seas and down the underside of the world. Little towns forgotten by the busy world
now, but able still to breed men and women who can take
hold of the world and shape it. And the day when such
towns will be needed in a troubled time may be close upon
us.

And a tough and smart and fine people are still the
chief crop along the Kennebec. There probably is more
unadulterated human nature to the square mile of this river
valley than in any other place I know. And it is this human
nature that shall be the chief burden of this book. For a
history of a place is no different from the toughness and
brightness of it people. These men and women have always
been many-sided creatures. They farmed while they fished,
hunted while they hayed, lumbered while they manufac-
tured, kept cows and chickens and horses while they built
ships and went around the world. And they were full of
sharp wisdom and tart proverbs, full of lustiness and unpu-
ritanic liveliness. They were cranky and independent and
witty all at once. They are still. I know one man whose
business is part fishing, part storekeeping, part farming,
but mostly philosophy. He will make a good chorus to my
book. These people of the Kennebec are people of the
heart of Maine and a book on their river cannot leave them
out.

And, finally, there is the scenery of the Kennebec. That
never changes. It will be there for poets and artists to feed
on tomorrow. The river comes down through some of the
loveliest of the earth's hills. The white pines flow silver in
the winds; the birches, which once furnished the chief craft
for the river, thrust white wonder up among the green. Islands like cut stone lie in the stream. Stone walls and roads
lean up high on the clouds. There is so much evergreen
that the leaves are never missed when they go. The snow
piles the valley deep with loveliness. Winter is as much a

wonder as summer. The fogs of Fundy come marching up its cool highway; in the heat and heart of summer, they move in like the lost continent of Atlantis on an August afternoon. The foghorn of Seguin, which is woven into the beginnings of my being and the beings of all the people by the Kennebec's mouth, wakes up and begins its nightlong chords. The white lighthouses of Seguin and Pond Island are snuffed out. The long parade of beauty, half a mile high, marches up the Kennebec. Little towns are lost and blotted out. Cows become only the chime of bells. And men along the river are shut in with their minds. It is a surprising thing. Maybe that is what makes them such interesting people to know. They get to know themselves. When October comes, the river flows through a forest fire of maples and oaks and birches and beeches, walls of color that no other river can show. The radiance of the leaves pours up into the sky. The clear sunshine is multiplied by light from within the trees. To go there is to go down the aisles of a bright dream.

There is a river!

# 2  Kennebec Weather

"On the 18th of Januarie they had in seven houres space thunder, lightning, raine, frost, snow, all in abundance, the last continuing."

This is, as far as I know, the earliest weather report in the Kennebec Valley. It was for the year 1608 and the place was the Popham Plantation. It reads mighty natural. It could be for the year 1937 just as well. The weather has not changed.

The Indians weren't the only things that tempered the steel of the Kennebec men. The weather did, too. Purchas's description is that of a good average day, the run-of-the-mill weather you can expect in seven Maine hours.

The weathervane always put on the top of the tallest pine tree is a necesary adjunct of a Kennebec farm. This is not for looks. It is to tell a man if there will be rain or hail, a thunderstorm or a fog, by the time he has the horses hitched. A farmer who begins his haying with that arrow pointing the wrong way may have to finish up his haying three farms away. A Maine farmer had always better take his winter coat along with him. A July scorcher winds up with three blankets and comforter on the bed at night. Many Kennebec men wear their long johns right through the summer. Woolen socks never go out of season with the lobstering men.

A Kennebec breeze can grow into a man-sized gale quicker that any other breeze going. It can get strong enough to lean on in an hour's time and it can rattle the teeth in your head and make your eyeballs jingle. No

wonder the Kennebec people took to sail early, with all
that power flying around loose. The winds get into people's minds; they get through the clapboards of the
stoutest houses; they get into people's sleep. My father
once had a farmhouse that he had to keep tied down with
chains over the roof, and he had to change the chains
when the winds veered. That's the kind of wind we raise in
Maine. The spruces grow close together so that all hands
of them can lean on each other and still be there in the
morning. The Kennebec men and women have learned to
fit their lives into the winds. Maybe their not having much
to say comes from the fact that they don't have a chance to
say it, in so much wind. They go with knees slightly bent
so as not to be surprised and turned bottom-side up. And
they go the right way to suit the blow. The Kennebec
sheep have heads raked like the funnels of oceangoing
steamers. Wind is a first-rate tonic, though. It can clean a
man's mind out well. A man coming in out of a wind is apt
to be pretty good to his children, I have noticed.

We raise pretty fair fogs up around the Kennebec. They
march up the river in August like Caesar's legions and
they push the world back inland for miles. They wipe away
islands and towns. The Kennebec cows have to be able to
navigate them when they come home from pasture and the
small Kennebec boys who follow their bells, as lobstering
men follow the bell buoy, have to carry a compass somewhere between their wide ears. August days may be only
two hours of sunlight long. I am surprised the Popham
colonists did not speak of the fog. There must have been
some that day.

You can't be sure of Maine weather. The farmers
reckon it lucky if they can get their beans in by Decoration
Day. Even then, June may turn out frosty. Any full moon is
sure to bring along a silver blanket that leaves the tomatoes
looking like the last slice of bacon on a side-slab. There's
one month, Maine folks say, when you can count on havin'
no frost. July. I believed that till last Fourth of July. I had
to set out my marigolds again after that.

It can rain harder along my river than any other place I
know. It isn't rain. It's an aerated waterfall. A sou'east rain

makes the windowpanes look like the walls of an aquarium. You expect to see a haddock look in on you any minute. But, then, a sou'wester is nothing to sneer at. It has given its name to the best Kennebec hat—with a long slope aft to keep the rain off the top joint of your spine if nowhere else. Oilskins are almost a national dress along the Kennebec. They are just as useful when plowing as when pulling lobster traps. It's raining pitchforks—that's an accurate Maine description for a lot of Maine weather.

Not that we don't have any snow. We do. Up to the eaves of the woodshed, and the boy has to walk through a canyon to fetch in his armful of birch and maple stovewood. Six feet of snow on the level is not a usual thing in Maine, because Maine is almost never level and the winds wouldn't let the snow lie there if it were. It snows that deep, but it all gathers round the tie-up to give the boys more to do to get the bull to the watering tub down a Grand Canyon of Carrara marble. Often you can recognize a farm by the cupola on the barn or the kitchen chimney smoking.

Snow is one thing. But cold is another. We have that, too. Cold enough to freeze the whiskers off a brass monkey, as the saying goes. Cold enough to go with a cane. Cold as Charity. Cold as the porridge at the poorhouse. Cold enough to stop a clock. Cold as slow molasses running uphill. There are a lot of Maine proverbs for cold. It is one of the best crops of the state.

When a Kennebec man goes to bed in winter he wears his wool socks, a flannel nightgown, perhaps his overcoat; he has two spruce-beer jugs filled with hot water for his feet, a hot flatiron for his back, and his complete supply of Boston *Transcripts* between mattress and springs. If he has a wife, he sends her along ahead of him to warm the bed. Likely as not, when he wakes up in the morning, there are icicles on his mustache, if he has one. When he gets up to light the fire for his wife and sings to keep his courage up, he sees his song right around him in the air.

By the last of March he may omit the flatiron.

It's not to be wondered at that Kennebec people are a tough crew. They've had to be to get through a Maine winter. The pindling ones perished before Wolfe captured Quebec.

But there's a bright side to all this. Apples that have a hard time in a brief summer, an acid soil, and an early frost, taste all the sweeter for that. "Sweet are the uses of adversity." The rigors of a spring day may clear the air until a man living along the Kennebec feels like a man living in the heart of a chandelier. And there are days in January, after an icestorm, for which chandelier is a pale word. It is like walking through a web of rainbows to be up and out in such a glory. Every bush coated with cut diamonds and the hills looking like the hills of the Apocalypse. It is a fine thing to be alive in such splendor, and the splendor of the days gets into a man; the splendor of nights so clear that the stars snap like sapphires overhead. The gulls go over washed whiter than snow. Cleanness and sharpness can put an edge on a man like a whetstone. It is the making of Maine's wit and sharpness of mind. It makes the Maine eyes their peculiarly true blue, and the people sparkle like their granite and snow. It powders homely  Yankee faces till they are handsome, and makes the corners of a man's eyes crinkle up, and he laughs in spite of death and taxes, zero weather, and everything.

There are days on the Kennebec, winter and summer, when the sky is so like crystal that you know you would strike the tone of an old goblet if you could reach high enough to flick it with your fingernail.

A person cannot live among these days and so much granite and pungent bayberry and sweet fern and clean evergreen without getting clear and goodsmelling inside. Bedrock living comes natural in a place where winds stir things to bedrock. A man can get used to loneliness when it is in so shining a place. The hardness of Kennebec winters and ledges is the hardness of peace and serenity.

# 3 Red Clay

The lantern swung back and forth in the low room with the force of the November gale that rocked the fisherman's small house to its foundation. Wings of dim light moved forward and back on the floor. The bitter-cold stars spattered the windowpanes. And high as the wind rose the full hymn of the Kennebec River as it ebbed out half-tide and met the southerly breakers of the Atlantic and pushed them back to sea.

It was a good night for a story of whales. The fisherman, who is also a philosopher and a wit, as most Maine fishermen are apt to be, was squatting on his oilskinned calves and letting himself right out. A few sons old enough to pull lobster traps at the Kennebec mouth were sitting around. Several others too small to own lobster traps were curled up asleep. A half dozen men with wrinkles at the corners of their eyes and windy eyebrows and mustaches were sitting back on heaps of seine and piles of lobster buoys, drinking in the best part of their whole day; the part they waited for even more eagerly than clams fried in batter and their willing wives. There was a stranger to the Maine coast listening, too, and he was the reason the philosopher at large put on the extra flourishes.

"Si, did she! There I lay and we was pulling in the cod pretty out there eastward of Seguin Light, me and them Massachusetts schoolmarms. They was flopping gurry all over my boat. And then one of the schoolmarms—the one with pretty brown hair—said to me, quiet-like, without raising her voice more'n a peg:

"'What would you say if I said I just saw a fish come up about ten times larger than this boat?'"

"'I'd say we'd better yank up our mudhook,' says I. And I got up on my hind legs and started pulling. I guess I started some stitches in me, I pulled that fast. I'd heard stories that summer.

"Moby Dick and me don't mix and he can have my part of the ocean!

"Just then I felt the whole piece of the Atlantic we was riding on in my 18-foot putt-putt lift up and then slide off slow. And a whale the size of a city block come up close enough so's I could have scratched him back of his ear with an oar. He blew when he see he'd missed us, playful-like, and we got a shower bath of a good part of the ocean.

"I threw the mudhook in and cranked my engine. She sneezed. And we started away from there proper. The schoolmarms was white as a sheet, but they didn't say nothing. I opened her up and we just bounced in toward Small Point Harbor.

"Then Moby Dick come up again, on the port this time, and this time you could count his eye winkers. We nearly turned over when we slid down that hill. I give her all the gas there was in the world. The schoolmarms was leaving their fingerprints on the gunwale.

"He come up ahead of us and I got a faceful when he waved good-bye with his flukes. They was about the size of my dory.

"'Playful, ain't he?' says I to the schoolmarms. They didn't open their heads. The engine went so fast our teeth rattled.

"He come up five times more before we got into shoal water, where he'd scratch the barnacles on his belly if he followed us. We got away. But I'm here to tell you there wasn't no gimp in the length of my pants when we got there safe. I just set. And the schoolmarms just set, too.

"'Moby Dick is right,' the little one with the brown fuzzy hair said, low and earnest. I looked to see if there was white streaks in her hair. Funny, but there wan't."

The fisherman scratched himself on his left ear.

"Tell them about the time the summer resorter asked you where you lived," piped up a big man with a bigger mustache.

"Oh, the Philadelphia gal? 'You see the bull spruce over there, marm?' I says to her. 'Well, that's where I roost nights. We lobstering men take to spruces natural-like.'"

"And what about the woman who wanted to know how often Maine fisherman die?"

"'Only once, marm,' I told her. 'Only once, and then they stop.'"

The outside door flew open and half of a whole gale came in. A tall boy came in along with it. The lantern gave a lurch and nearly blew out.

"Jehosaphat! Take it easy, Bill. Do you want to turn the whole house upside down? Shut that door to!"

The extra son pushed the door to with his back. He had the mudflats still on him. He walked over to the table and threw down a long brown thing.

"See what I got clamming. Dug it up out of that old shell heap on Back Bay."

The boy's father picked up the brown thing.

"Some old boy's femur," he said. "And golly! That was a man to fill up a pair of pants! Must have stood six-six in his stocking feet."

The philosopher held the bone up to the light. It was brown as an oak leaf in November and it flaked to dust where he nicked it with his thumbnail. "Been there in that gravel a long time. Look, see!" He broke the long bone in two like a straw. He took up one end and ran his fingers over the knobs lovingly. He riddled off all the Latin names for the femur's protuberances.

The stranger in their midst sat up and took notice. He wasn't used to Maine fishermen. He did not know that most of them have more than one string to their bow. He had not expected to find an authority on human anatomy in this fishing place. He did not know that this philosopher-fisherman had pored over Gerrish's *Anatomy* till he knew it by heart.

The philosopher went on showing off and shooting off steam for the stranger's benefit.

"*Linea aspera, peroneal trochanter, tibial trochanter, posterior intertrochanteric* ridge ... Godfrey!" the reciter called out suddenly. "They souped him!"

The femur bone had been cooked. A long gash had
been cut near the end of the bone to draw off the marrow.

"Good God!" said the stranger. "Who was it?"

"Well," the philosopher said slowly. "That'd take a
mighty smart feller to figure out. Rodney Jasper maybe.
Your guess is as good's mine. You see, he's been cooked
and eaten a good long time."

"How do you know that?"

"Because he's one of them Oyster Shell People and
they got through with the bones in that shell bank Bill
here dug into somewheres around ten thousand years
ago."

"The Oyster Shell People?"

"Yes." Cap'n Cy Bibber pulled down his jumper and
settled himself back on his heels. "Them Oyster Shell
People was the old-time settlers on the Kennebec. You dig
them up now and then when you go clamming 'round
here. Their bones ain't much, they go to pieces quick
when the air strikes them. But their teeth are still good.
Better'n yours and mine right this minute. You get a lot of
good teeth out of them shell pits. Did you see any teeth,
Bill?"

"No, wan't any sign of a skull or anything."

"Them Oyster Shell boys was old-timers, all right. But
they wan't the first settlers on the Kennebec. There was
folks here before them. The Red Paint People."

"Red Paint?"

"Yes, sir. They was the real old-timers. They fished for
herring here more thousands of years ago than I've got fingers and toes. And my daddy saw to it that I got the regu-
lation number."

"Where does the red paint come in?"

"Oh, that? That's the red stuff you always find around
where you find their graves. Looks like a lump of red ocher
or red clay. You may find arrowheads and axes, or you may
not. But you always find that. Their bones didn't last out.
But their paint is just as fresh as the day they took it into
their graves. It sticks to your hands and it don't come off
easy. The scientific fellers say it's iron oxide. But they don't
know what it was for. The red stuff is always there. Maybe

it's something to do with some god or other they had. Maybe it's something to do with a man. Sort of gets you thinking someway. Red, like a man. Like blood. They must have dipped down deep somewheres or other to get stuff red as that. Red, like a man's blood. Hard to get off your hands. Like blood."

# 4 Good Eating Begins in Maine

The first settlers on the banks of the Kennebec were Stone Age men. Nobody knows what race they were, where they came from, or where they went. They were fishers and hunters, that we know, as all Kennebec men have been down to today. They may have dredged up oysters and speared the salmon and sturgeon, they may have made love in the brief, fierce summers of Maine and looked at sunsets that are woven on no looms of weather save those of the evergreen coasts, they may have waged wars and lived and died here for thirty thousand years. Perhaps the clear blue river was worked into their being deeper than in any of the dewdrop people who have shone only briefly by the Kennebec since their day. They belong to the time before the sun was up.

Yet now and then, at Carratunk and elsewhere, a few things they left turn up like flakes of the morning stars. And we know that they brought down the caribou with small flints delicately sculptured as the petals on a daisy. We know they took loveliness in their hands when they went out with strings of rawhide to fling about the slim legs of running deer, for the stones that weighted the ends of the string are proportioned as exquisitely as Greek vases and their sides are graven with threefold patterning as right as the cusps of a lotus flower. When they took the skins off their quarry, they did it with stone knives tapered and hollowed as thin as the shell of the freshwater clam. When they ran through the ancient evergreens, they wore around their necks a hundred young new moons, slim crescents of

blue stone pierced twice for the rawhide that bound them
all together. They learned lovely shapes from the sun and
moon and trees. These are small words out of the night,
but eloquent ones, and words of a universal language.

Tools can tell the story of a race as surely as temples.
These primitive Kennebec men were artists. Their artifacts
are considered the finest of the whole Stone Age. Loveliness helped them win their food, as it helps their modern
kinsmen; the artists who learn symmetry today from the
birds and the leaves and the trees along the great river.

And there is the mystery that is dug up always with the
dust of their bones—the red clay. Scientists can tell you the
exact spot where those ancient Maine men found the iron
oxide: on the slope of Katahdin, the mountain that sits in
the heart of Maine and pours out the great Penobscot. But
they cannot tell you whether this color was used for deco-
rating the body or embalming the dead, to keep the color
of life among the bones, or whether it was a thing having
to do with a lost religion. Perhaps it links the earliest Kennebec men to the extinct Beothuks of Newfoundland, who
smeared their bodies with it and were called Red Indians
and Red-skinned, or Red-painted, people by the first European codfisherfolk who saw them in the sixteenth century.
The clay is found in lumps or smeared over the bottoms of
graves there and in Massachusetts and on Lake Champlain,
as well as in Maine.

From graves in the earth, the Kennebec's story passes
on to monuments rising high above it, from the Red Paint
People to another lost race, the Oyster Shell Men. The
mementos that these latter have left us suggest that, unlike
their beauty-loving predecessors, it was the flesh rather
than the spirit that profited them. They were epicures and
gluttons.

The largest monuments to human hunger in all the
world are in the Kennebec region—heaps of oyster shells
that represent thousands of years of fine eating. There are
some shell banks along the Kennebec, but they are thickest
on the tidal Damariscotta River, one of the many indenta-
tions of the sea that lace the Kennebec mouth to the east.
Here, on both sides of the water, they form cliffs 25 feet

high. One such heap is over a hundred rods square, and
this cenotaph to man's appetite contains 45 million cubic
feet of oyster shells. These shell mounds are rather curi-
ously grouped, and some people believe that their arrange-
ment had some religious significance. Maybe they are temples to the God Gastronomy! He is one of the oldest of
our deities.

Around this largest of man's dining tables, ancient men
and women sat and rose so many notches nearer heaven as
the centuries went by and their table and chairs grew under
them. Their cloth was always white. Today's dinner was always waiting in the water below; they had only to dish it
up. A page of history, for once, reads like a chronicle of
Elysium. When the world is so full of pyramids and tombs
and triumphal arches to man's cruelty, it is good to have
such jovial memorials as these shell banks. Sometimes,
though, diggers come upon human skulls and other bones
even here. But I like to believe that their owners reassigned
them willingly, having eaten too many oysters to survive
their joy! The old bones crumble when exposed to the air,
and only the teeth that accounted for the ancient shellfish
survive.

These, the arrowheads, and the spoons and dishes that
always are lost at banquets, have outlasted their owners and
the years. Copper spoons and shards of pottery and celts of
fine workmanship tell in a few simple lines the tale of a
highly advanced culture, in which eating was not the least
of the arts. It is an elegiac note, warning us that the world
does not always move forward to better things.

Not even the thing in nature. Many of these
Damariscotta shells that have survived the creatures who
built and the creatures who ate them are larger than oysters known now. Purchas, in *His Pilgrimage,* says that the
colonists sent out by Sir John Popham found "oysters
nine inches in length: and were told that on the other side
they were twice as great." So the shellfish were still there
in 1607 and the red men had inherited the old banquet
tables.

But the oysters are gone now. Some change in the seasons, perhaps, swept the food of tens of thousands of years

out of existence; or some more subtle revolution in the
sea's housekeeping, like that which has obliterated all the
eelgrass in the Maine bays since I was a boy spearing floun-
ders there, and now brought back the quahaugs that had
disappeared almost completely for two decades.

The only two oyster beds in Maine in recent times that
I know of were the oyster pavilion across the bay from my
father's farm, where thick-mustached Victorian beaux in
plaid vests ate themselves groggy on imported oysters, and
the sad attempt of the Bureau of Fisheries to plant oysters
in Buttermilk Creek. Cap'n Cy Bibber, the fisherman-
philosopher at large and my authority on the human
anatomy, likes to tell what became of that experiment:

"You see, my friend, Cap'n Stover, he got to worrying
about them poor oysters out there in Buttermilk. It bothered him nights. He knew what the ice would do to them
shellfish when it made in the winter. It would freeze onto
the oysters and lift them right out of their warm beds and
carry them out into deep water and drown them. It wor-
ried Cap'n Stover terrible. So when it came on November,
he went out and took them all in. You can still see the
shells round his back doorstep. Cap'n Stover always had
the name of being a softhearted man. Yes, sirree!"

# 5  The Dawn People

When the first navigators from Europe nosed their way up the Kennebec, the tall, handsome Abenakis were the people who gathered with the starry-eyed deer to see them go past.

The Abenakis called themselves The Dawn People and they were very sure they had owned the Kennebec River from the creation of the world, when it had been handed to them, bright and new as a dewdrop, from the hands of the Great Master of Life. They were also certain that they were the best tribe of the whole Algonkin family. They were not the simple children of nature that Europeans were expecting to find in the forest of the New World. They were part Caliban and part Ariel; perhaps in equal proportions, until the best in the Europeans brought out the wolf and the fox in them. They did not live off a rich land without effort, lying at ease beside steams and trees that spread banquets at their feet. They were a lean and hungry, hard-bitten people. They were great hunters and fishers. They had to work for the right of inhabiting the banks of the Kennebec, as later Kennebec men had to do. It has always been a river that made men.

Half the year was white hunger, with the salmon and sturgeon locked under crystal, the deer and moose walled round with snow. Fire and food were precious, slender things. The Indians treasured food in holes in the earth, in smoky houses of bark and skin, dried food, smoked food, concentrated food. They had learned to carry the red seeds of life that meant a safe home in a snowdrift, and a camp-fire and cooking. They carried fire smoldering in a fungus punk, shut up in a clamshell artfully cased in clay. Each

man had slung at his belt a small hot god ready to spring
up tall and save him. And all the men had the feet of winter on their backs, ready to be added to their own. Purchas
describes them: "They have a kind of shooes a yard long,
fourteene inches broad, made like a Racket, with strong
twine or sinews of a Deere; in the mids is a hole wherein
they put their foote, buckling it fast." On such feet, built
of the forest and creatures in it, the Abenakis lived half
their lives.

The Dawn People venerated their ancestors, respected
their women, and loved their children above all posses-
sions. They had come close to the Dorian institution of the
love of man for man, the forerunner of Platonic love. The
Abenakis lived and died paired off as friends. Such friend-
ships cut across miles and years and clans. A man's *nidoba*
was more than a brother, he was the breath of his ribs, and
a man laid down his life gladly for him. These red men
had a fine system of administering justice.

Twice a year, in October, before going off to Moosehead for the winter's huntings, and in spring, on their
return to feasts of fish, they sat in council on Swan Island
and other council islands, and the sagamores stood up and
smoothed out the wrinkles in their lives, holding life and
death in their hands. They owned their lands in common.
Deeds of sale and private ownership were unknown,
though hunting rights could be bartered. That fact was to
be the cause of a hundred years of bloodshed, screams of
agony in the night, and whole English villages wrapped in
flames.

The Dawn People had houses. No one could live outdoors along the Kennebec during seven months of the
year. The Abenakis built bark cabins, long houses with
ridgepoles, and small ones around a central paved fireplace.
They had towns made up of large groups of dwelling
houses in regular streets, as at Norridgewock and at
Koussinok, where Hallowell now stands. And they built
boats. Birch-bark canoes, some of them large enough to
hold a small army of men. Even before the sunrise, Kennebec men were builders of boats. It was in the blood.
And they could sail their boats, through the teeth of the
rapids of the upper river, among the tall towers of the

Atlantic waves out past Monhegan, where swam whales big
as the world.

These Kennebec men were artists, too, in dressing
skins, in making clothes, weapons, and basketry, in drawing
pictographs. They communicated over long distances not
only by the skin drums that talked along the Kennebec
from Moosehead to Monhegan, but by pictures and geometric designs.

Like most other Indian tribes, they fought in small
bands, in fierce secrecy, knife in one hand and tomahawk in
the other, deadly as bobcats trailing the deer. But they also
had plenty of play; sports of wrestling, running and jumping, and intricate games of ball. They had agriculture. They
raised beans and squash and maize. They knew the science
of fertilizing the land. They heaped alewives at the edge of
their villages to rot and mellow. And a ripe alewife went
under each hill of corn. They had hoes and their women
knew how to use them, hilling the earth around the green
fingers of life. Yankee farmers today work the same acres
that the Indians opened to the sun along the Kennebec
and eat the popcorn that is descended from the ears that
hung in husks to dry in the Indian wigwams of five hundred years ago.

The Dawn People had religion, too. They knew there
was something behind the music of the running river and
the song of the pines. That something was a great warrior
and a great lover of life, and he had the sun and the moon
and the stars around his strong neck. He was in a man's
thigh when his body sang over the snow on shoes that
could outrace the deer.

God lived up near where the Kennebec began, among
the mountains. You could see something like his head if
you looked up at snowy Katahdin. But you did not look up
there much and you kept away from his rocky feet and
legs. For if you went too near to the house of the Spirit,
there would come a rushing and a roaring; after that there
would be nothing else to tell, and your children would
have to live by the hunting of another man. Civilized men
may smile and murmur "snowslides and avalanches." But
the Abenaki knew what he knew.

One day, ages before, a smart Abenaki girl went too

high up Katahdin after the big blueberries. Katahdin
roared down and no girl came home that night. Some
years later, though, a beautiful matron with a strange smile
came down from the mountain and a handsome young
sannup ran at her side. He had queer eyebrows. They
looked like edges of the gray granite. But he was as good
to look at as a mountain in dogwood time. The boy was
handy around the village, too, for whatever he pointed his
finger at froze into death. A useful lad in the hunt! All
went well for years and the tribe waxed fat and saucy on
the easy kills of game, but a black day came and the youth
fell in to anger at his own grandfather in the hunt. He
pointed his finger at the old man, and the grandfather
dropped like a stone. The braves lifted up their voices in
wrath, for the old man was their best snowshoe maker.
They turned on the youth of the granite eyebrows and
chased him into the forest. But when they were hot on his
heels, the heavens split with a crack and the earth rocked
under them. Spruces 50 feet high went down like splinters.
When the air cleared, the boy was gone and Katahdin was
staring them in the face through the wreck of the forest.
The men stole home. The boy who might have made a
mighty chief was never again seen among men. But everyone knows that he was with his father, on Katahdin. He
would be at home up there where he belonged.

Life was hard and uncertain for The Dawn People. But
two things they had to comfort them and make life a well-
spring of wonder forever; two things that men still enjoy
along the Kennebec. Bayberry candles and tobacco. Above
the delights of a marriage bed of balsam, above children
and family and songs, there were tapers a foot long that
carried the smell of summer into the midst of winter, smell
of fragrant Maine that early mariners caught miles out at
sea, and the smell and taste of that plant which has done
more to ease man on through life than religion itself, the
plant that Sir Walter Raleigh tasted, to compose his spirits,
just before he went to his death. And they smoked their
Maine tobacco in the big claw of a Maine lobster. Bayberry, tobacco, lobster. What more could a man ask? So,
fortified with bayberry and nicotine, the Abenakis held the

Kennebec many thousand strong, a tough and bright people. But another race of men was coming to fit their bodies
into the winds and to be made tough and bright and smart
by the splendors and the rigors of Maine weather.

# 6  The First Families of the Kennebec

Whoever it was with European blood in his veins that first feasted his eyes on the fine point lace of Maine firs with the mountains behind them, who first saw the enamel blue of the Kennebec River running through a light like that inside a cut crystal, will probably never be known. Maybe in was St. Brendan. He sailed west for forty days and got an eyeful of strange lands that were like the doorstep to paradise. But whoever it was that came first, he certainly, as Maine folks put it, saw a sight for sore eyes. It isn't every day that a man can sail into the lower end of a rainbow or into a river like crushed diamonds. If he came in the winter, he got more of an eyeful than he would have got in the summer. For dark evergreen and snow add to the natural luster of Maine.

Maybe it was a Viking. Leif Ericsson got down lower than Maine, likely. And no seafarer would ever have passed the Maine coast by. Not if he had eyes in his head or a nose for fragrant odors. Maybe it was an even older European than a Nordic. On Manana, the island next to Monhegan, near the Kennebec's mouth, there is a rock that bears what seems to be an inscription. Perhaps it is an old Indian pictograph, though some people believe it to be a runic message of the Vikings; other people say it was put there by the Phoenicians, the men who founded Cadiz in Spain and colonies in Britain. Such good sailors might have sailed as far west as the cod banks of the Kennebec's mouth. Anyway, fishermen were here early and stayed late. They found the water alive with cod and could dip them up by the bucketful. The cod, not Columbus, opened the

door to a new world. There were whales too, brushing the
steep sides of Monhegan; big as islands themselves, Hakluyt describes them. There was good fishing everywhere.
Fishermen were the first families on the Kennebec.

French fishers in little craft were found off the Kennebec in fleets by the early English explorers. A dozen or
so little fishing boats calmly loading in the cod and hake—
that was what Englishmen found at the doorsteps of
Norumbega, the incredible crystal utopia that they sought.
It was disconcerting to the great navigators to come upon
everyday Europeans fishing quietly here; but men are not
likely to tell everybody where the fish bite best. They
weren't then any more than they are now. At Pemaquid
there are drying floors for fish made of paving stones that
some archaeologists claim came from sixteenth-century St.
Augustine.

At any rate, Columbus had hardly stumbled upon San
Salvador before high European ships were poking their
noses along the coast of Maine, hunting for the Northwest
Passage to India and lands where jewels lay like so many
pebbles for the picking up. John and Sebastian Cabot
sailed past and claimed Newfoundland and all the coast behind down to Cape Cod for Henry VII, in 1497. Then in
1524 and 1534 came Cartier and the French; they claimed
the same region and called it New France. So were sown
the seeds of an international blood feud. And thousands of
future lives were doomed to torture and death, lives from
the Kennebec, too. Cartier saw Indians as white as men in
France. Probably European fishermen had already been active in domestic affairs. The French brought settlers over
to the Gulf of St. Lawrence. Trappers, traders, fishermen,
and missionaries were soon living as neighbors to the red
men. Henry Hudson may have thrust his nose into the
Kennebec. The Frenchmen from the St. Lawrence certainly
did, and were soon yanking the Kennebec salmon and sturgeon into their boats as if they belonged there. Other nations came, too, for it was a paradise for fish. In the year
1583, Sir Humphrey Gilbert counted thirty-six English,
French, Spanish, and Portuguese ships fishing off Newfoundland. Sir Walter Raleigh—who had dreamed of

mating with Gloriana, who was Gloriana's "shepherd of
the ocean," and who spoke broad Devon to his dying
day—came coasting down, explored the Maine shore
and claimed it and all the eastern coast for Elizabeth, the
Virgin, as Virginia.

Surely one of the first Englishmen to swim the
Kennebec, and half a hundred other rivers from Mexico
to Maine, was David Ingram, the most famous walker of
American history. He was the sole survivor of a hundred
English seamen marooned by Captain Hawkins in the
Gulf of Mexico in 1558. Ingram decided to walk home to
England. He walked along the coast of Florida and then
headed north. The Indians bothered him a little here and
there, but he got to know them and played a peculiar kind
of game with them. The point of the game was to run
northeast. Ingram was a good runner. He left his playmates
behind him, and started a new game of the same kind
among the next Indians.

He walked all the way to the Penobscot. There he
found a French fishing ship, hard by the fabled Norumbega of Indian lore. He had been to visit Norumbega and
had seen pearls by the bucketful, pillars of crystal and silver, and furs bright enough to blind a man. He had seen
an even brighter thing—Maine under snow. He told the
Frenchmen about the pearls. They were all for going after
them, but David said no. They must get a big ship first.
They must go back to Europe. So he got the Frenchmen
to ferry him the rest of the way home. David Ingram certainly saw more of America than did any other man in his
century.

David got to England at last. And the dream of great
treasure and great empire spread like wildfire through
England. Englishmen had no idea that America was so big
until Ingram walked across it. Great captains were closeted
with Gloriana—Davis and Sir Walter Raleigh, Simon
Ferdinando and Sir Humphrey Gilbert. Secret maps were
drawn, a continent was partitioned out. And behind all
these activities was the last of the medieval alchemists, Dr.
Dee, who pulled the wool over Gloriana's eyes for many
years. Dee had his hands in mysterious red powers from

Wales that would change all things into gold and his head
was full of schemes about the New World. But the gold
and crystal cities faded; only the bitter northern Strait of
Davis gave promise of passage to the riches of the Indies.
Norumbega faded out into trackless forests full of a solider
wealth of timber and furs and into waters alive with fish,
fish enough to feed the world.

In the first years of the seventeenth century, when
European navigators were ceasing to look for cities of
crystal and diamonds, and Ariels and Calibans under every
American tree, and were beginning to think in terms of
bread and butter and how they could make utopia pay,
the Englishmen, Bartholomew Gosnold in 1602 and
Martin Pring in 1603, under the aegis of the new Virginia
Company, explored Penobscot Bay. And in 1604, the
Frenchmen, De Monts and Champlain, settled the land of
Acadia and sowed the first European grain on the new
continent. They visited the Kennebec, looking for the
seeds of wild wheat that the Indians cultivated. They gave
Monhegan its second name in one year. And in 1605, in
the merry month of May, just ahead of Champlain, came
Captain George Weymouth in the good ship *Archangel*,
looking for the Northwest Passage and the wealth of the
Indies, or Norumbega anyway, and found something better. He found something closer to paradise—Maine in full
bloom. He sailed into the heart of the crystal that is
Maine.

He found Monhegan Island first, the jewel of all coast
artists to come, called it St. George's for Merry England,
and then burst into the Kennebec. He found harbors by
the dozen, each big enough to hold the whole British navy
—he called one of them Pentecost; and he found such fish
as dreams are made of: "Plenty of salmon and other fishes
of great bigness, good lobsters, rock-fish, plaice, and
lumps, and, with two or three hooks enough of cod and
haddock to supply the ship's company for three days." He
found "great muscles" too, one having fourteen pearls in
it. He went into ecstasies over the trees. Here was God's
plenty, and here were the riches that were to make the
Kennebec one of the arteries of a new nation. Captain

George sowed peas and barley and in sixteen days they were eight inches tall, the soil was that fertile. George and his men rolled in milk and honey. They sailed up bays and rivers in all directions. One fine June day, when the Maine thrushes were in full cry, the English sailors, all in armor and with a small boy to tote their powder and match, rowed a shallop up into an Elysium with Maine pines holding up the summer clouds. They landed and walked a piece, then they set up a cross, knelt down, sweating in their armor, and thanked God. Well they might, for they had explored the finest river of Maine—The Kennebec. They went back toward the *Archangel* feeling like gods. They were the first of a long line of Kennebec men to feel so. Kennebec men have felt so ever since. After they had thanked God, the men went fishing. They probably all went in swimming, too. It was the right time of year, for Maine, and there was a boy along.

Weymouth and his Archangelites did some real trading in Maine. They swapped some gewgaws worth five shillings for forty skins of beaver, otter, and sable. It was the beginnings of a century when every gentlemen in Europe had to wear North America on his head in a beaver hat. These traders were making an early start in the business of the future. In spite of the exhortations of the Dean of Paul's that the men of the Virginia Company should be more eager to trade a catechism than a knife or hatchet for the wealth of America, and bring back good news of so many conversions instead of so many shiploads of lumber and spices, the English traders were more interested in sassafras and furs than in souls.

Navigators could smell Maine far out at sea. No wonder, with so much bayberry and sweet fern around. The poet Drayton knew his Maine:

> When as the luscious smell
> Of that delicious land,
>   Above the seas that flows,
>   The clear wind throws,
> Your hearts to swell
> Approaching the dear strand ...

> O you the happiest men,
> Be frolic then!
> Let cannons roar ...

The English explorers had a nose for the "useful sassafras" and pine and fish. The herbs of Maine alone drew
them like magnets. Of course, they would be glad to pick
up pearls and gold, if they came on them in "Virginia,
earth's only paradise." But the first sailors to the Kennebec
were thinking about breeding a new race of heroes, too.
They foresaw that this wealthy world would be a fine cradle for men of a future empire. Drayton had told them
about it:

> And in regions far,
> Such heroes bring ye forth
>     As those from whom we came,
>     And plant our name
> Under that star
> Not known unto our North . . .

They found the sassafras. The heroes were to come
later.

Once England had gotten to know the Kennebec, it
was not long before Englishmen were coming to settle. In
May 1607, the Plymouth Company, which had taken over
North Virginia as the London Company had taken over
South Virginia in 1606, sent out the first English colony
to North America at the Kennebec's mouth. They built
where the Kennebec roared out into the open Atlantic.
The expedition had been started by the Lord Chief Justice
of England, Sir John Popham, who had got his estate from
a nobleman who was glad to trade it for his neck.

Aubrey says the Kennebec colony was stocked "out of
all the gaols of England." There were a hundred men and
two ships; the *Mary and John*, captained by Raleigh
Gilbert, whose name is still on the promontory of Long
Island, and the *Gift of God*, commanded by Captain
George Popham, kinsman of the Chief Justice. They built
a fort, St. George's, got out their fishing lines, built fifty
houses, and dug themselves in for the winter. They had

religion along in the person of Richard Seymour, an Episcopalian clergyman, and they built him a church. So the
first Protestant service in America was Episcopalian, not
Puritan, and it was celebrated thirteen years before the pilgrims sang psalms at Plymouth.

After they got settled, the Popham colonists went
exploring. They sailed up the Kennebec, through
Merrymeeting Bay, came to the island in the falls of the
Androscoggin where Brunswick now stands, hauled their
boat up by a rope over the first fall but could not get it
over the second. So they explored the Brunswick plains.
"They found the Countrey stored with Grapes white and
red, good Hops, Onions, Garlike, Okes, Walnuts, the soile
good." They went back to their village rejoicing.

The winter was one of the robust kind, such as only
Maine can grow. These first Kennebec men took in their
belts and scrabbled for food. It was hard sledding. Popham
died. The colonists may have been rapscallions, but they
could use tools. They built a ship of thirty tons during the
winter and named her the *Virginia of Sagadahoc*. This was
the first ship built by Englishmen in the New World. It
was the first of a long line of ships that were to go out of
Kennebec's mouth and whiten all the world with their
sails.

At year's end, half the colonist's packed up and went
home. They took the *Virginia* with them. The vessel finished its days, with good Englishmen chained in it, among
the Barbary pirates. But fifty-five Englishmen stayed in
Maine. Whatever became of these colonists nobody knows.
They were not at Popham when the next comers landed.
But there are foundations of houses around Pemaquid that
no one can explain. Monhegan was probably, even this
early, more or less continuously inhabited by English fishermen. The Pophamites may have gone out there or joined
the Indians. By all accounts, they were tough customers
and could have made their beds anywhere. Very likely they
stayed on this side of the Atlantic and were the original settlers, instead of the men of Jamestown of 1607.

Maine has her mystery of lost colonists as Virginia has
hers. The Kennebec keeps her secrets as does the James.

Tradition says that this was not the only time a Maine
town got lost. The people left behind when the men of
Waldoboro sailed away to attack Louisburg, a century and
a half later, were not there when the soldiers retuned. No
sign of a struggle, nothing broken, the plates on the table,
and yet not a soul of them was ever seen again.

That same year, 1607, the French settled at Mt.
Desert, planted gardens, and made friends with the Indians. So began the century-and-a-half race between two
nations for the land of Maine; a race that did not end until
the forests were flecked with blood, a thousand Englishmen had had the experience of walking to Quebec as prisoners, and Wolfe and Montcalm ended the feud with their
lives on the Plains of Abraham.

After Popham collapsed, the English fishermen re-
sumed their place as the first families of the Kennebec. The
year 1614 saw Captain John Smith, trailing clouds of glory
and Turks' heads he had bagged on the Danube, come
awhaling to the mouth of the river. He built seven boats at
Monhegan, took lessons in harpooning leviathan from the
Indians, looked for silver mines, and explored the coast
down to Cape Cod. He made a map of the region, and
named the land New England.

By 1615, the coast around the Kennebec was studded
with fishing settlements. There were traders, too, and rapscallions of the first water seeking new fields. Nobody will
ever know how many English people were homesteading in
Maine before Plymouth was even imagined. Many Maine
settlers were men who did not care to put an address on
their calling cards. They had no ambition to get into history books. Maine began not in the state of grace, but as
fine hunting and fishing grounds with fat in the spider and
the goose hung high. Life there was jovial, and a lusty crew
lived without ministers, or with only the Anglican kind.
And, by the same token Maine human nature was never
cut to the Puritanic pattern of straitness and narrowness.
The Presbyterian and Congregational ministers did not
settle themselves solidly on the Kennebec communities
till along about the time of the Revolution. Maine got a
fairly robust start without them. And the generous design

in living of the sea-captain families had its beginning in the
beginnings of Maine. They were a mixed crowd, these first
families: English, French, Dutch, and Spanish.
Monhegan was a general European fishing port two
years before Plymouth began. In 1618, a mutinous crew of
Englishmen, from a ship sent out by Sir Ferdinando
Gorges, walked up to the Kennebec from the Saco, got
out to Monhegan, and built a village. The earlier settlers
on the island had, by this time, moved to the mainland at
Pemaquid. Monhegan was "a settlement of some beginnings" by 1621. And when the Pilgrims at Plymouth
scraped the bottom of their corn bin in 1622 and starvation stared them in the face, Monhegan fed them fat, loading them down with fish. And Monhegan would not take
any money for it. Here was another instance of the famous
Maine hospitality. Later, Governor Winslow wrote: "I
found kind entertainment and good respect with a willing-
ness to supply our wants, which was done, so far as able,
and would not take any bills for the same, but did what
they could freely." Monhegan Island was a seedbed for the
mainland. Sturdy inhabitants moved over to start new
colonies. A John Brown bought himself an estate for fifty
skins from the Indians at Pemaquid and his heirs held it till
1812. Before 1623, there were flourishing settlements
along the Kennebec, at Sagadahoc (now Bath), and at
Merrymeeting, which is like its name and the finest bay in
Christendom.

Sir Ferdinando Gorges was the ruler of the new vast
estate that was developing from day to day. He got his
patent from the Plymouth Company to all the land between the Piscataqua and the Kennebec, and ruled it like a
king. Families bred themselves big on the islands, shipped
across, and went singing up the wilderness on both sides of
the Kennebec. There were fish and fur and lumber, corn
and maple syrup, geese that darkened the sun of spring,
ducks in islands among the reaches of Merrymeeting.
Cabins sprang up on every point. By 1634, the masts for
the ships of the Royal Navy were being cut along the
Kennebec, tall white pines marked with the arrow of the
king. In 1635, there were, not counting fishermen and

trappers and traders, almost 150 families set up in steady
housekeeping by the Kennebec. It was as flourishing a
young empire as ever kicked up its heels under the blue
sky. The winters were hard as diamonds, but the people
were tough and stayers. The weak ones died off or left.
The water and woods were full of food for men who could
come and get it. Get it they did, and grew fat and saucy.

In 1639, that empire got its final name: the Province
of Maine. It spread out to the east and threatened the
French settlements. Other colonies cast envious eyes on it.
In 1664, the Duke of York, having stolen New Amsterdam
and Delaware from the Dutch, took over Maine from the
Kennebec to the St. Croix. He even pastured some of the
fat, comfortable Dutch burghers of New York up here
where men grew lean and ran themselves down to withing.
After the first shock of surprise, they ran themselves as lean
and lithe as any. During the next twenty-five years, Maine
passed through various hands; France, New York, and
Massachusetts ruling in turn. It was a luscious morsel
tossed about among upstart later colonies. After the Indian
wars, Massachusetts picked up the smoking ruins of Maine
and kept the Kennebec until the Missouri Compromise of
1820.

But the people prospered no matter who the ruler was.
The same story was repeated in hundreds of small chapters:
a clearing among the pines, corn planted, vegetables raised
and garnered into earth cellars such as the Indians used,
fish dried on flakes, women spinning, men digging out
stumps, small families widening in their circle around the
hearth as the years went by, new young men carrying the
coals of home to new hearths, new troops of boys in
homespun driving cows to slender pastures between the
walls of the forest, axes ringing, men singing and breeding,
and every autumn the chimneys smoking farther up the
Kennebec, to the first waterfalls.

And something like the hand of Providence moved in
the wilderness to give this young empire fifty good years in
which to grow and get on its feet. In 1615, the Indians of
the Penobscot and the eastern Abenakis fell afoul of each
other in war. The Kennebec red men got the worst of it

and were badly weakened by slaughter and famine. And
then, in the winter of 1617–1618, a mysterious disease,
harmless to the whites, swept the whole race of red men
from the Penobscot to Cape Cod. It may have been just
the measles or some offspring of the family of common
colds. But it was fatal to the sons of the forest who ran
naked in the summers and had never had colds before.
Probably three-quarters of all the Abenakis were dead by
spring. Men came upon whole villages of whitening bones.
Had the great host of Indians lived, the story might have
been different in the next century, in the Indian wars, but
the doom of the red race had already been sealed before
the battle for a continent began.

# 7 "An Up and Coming Lot"

It was a wicked cold night. The frost sparkled at the corners of all the panes in the fishhouse.

Cap'n Cy Bibber took his corncob out of his mouth. He spat across the room to the grate in the barrel stove and hit it clean as a whistle.

"Yes, sirree! Them first Yankees on the Kennebec," Cy said, "was an up-and-coming lot, I'm telling you. The Old Boy in them bigger'n a woodchuck. Swing your partners and ladies' chain! And they wan't fussy how many ladies they had. The more the merrier. And they needed plenty young cut-me-downs to snake out the codfish and slit them open to dry.

"They was great ones for their grub. Home wan't home without two deer hanging up, smokehouse full of fat alewives, six pigs with their spareribs sprung open, a hogshead of hulled corn, a tierce of molasses, a dozen hams, ten barrels of halibut heads, six buckets of tongues and sounds, maple syrup enough to swim in, and dried cod enough to cover a three-acre lot. Apple pie and tea all turned out! Sweet Beulah Land!

"They was traders from way back, too, and would swap their grandmother for a mess of yellowbelly eels.

"They give the Injuns some ten-cent store strings of beads and moved in on their land and made themselves right to home. First thing John Henry Injun knew, they was in his tent and tying on his snowshoes, rolling up in his pelts, and dipping into his fat. And the Injun was out in the cold with nothing but his shirt and pants left. Next day, they swapped the Injun some Christmas-tree gewgaws, and got the shirt and pants.

"They was smart people.

"Injun began to catch on after he'd lost even his eye-teeth. But he woke up too late, and had to mum it without any teeth.

"Then the Injun got mad and started collecting hair. But the Yankees went into the hair business, too. Injun didn't have no show. The Yankee could snowshoe circles around him, shin faster up a tree, paddle a canoe right by him as though he was hitched. He was more of an Injun than the Injun was himself. He had learnt all the Injun tricks, even to smoking a pipe. He could shoot the buttons off the Injun's shirt while the Injun was drawing a bead. So the Injuns pulled in their horns and curled up their toes. They was through. They knew a better Injun when they saw one.

"The Yankees was great fellers for stone walls. They strung them all over the country. Smart as a whip. 'Here, boys,' they'd say to their platoon of sons, 'while you're resting, lay us up a mile or two of stone wall.' And their sons went right out and did it. Their daddies laid back and did the heavy planning, smoking a corncob the way they'd learnt from the Injuns. Then after the boys was rested, they let them set up a barn or two before supper.

"They was smart, no getting round it."

# 8 A Century of
## Agony and Fire

The Kennebec empire of contented and strong
men sang along the forest. But the song was about to be
silenced in those snug houses that looked out on the blue,
moving highway of life.

The history of the Kennebec River from 1675 until the
Revolution is a history of houses standing in flames and
feet running desperately through the night. It is a story of
women and little children walking the long aisle of the forest in the dead of winter to Quebec. A tale of horrible fires
and human figures in them and of dark devils dancing
about the blaze.

Two races from two different planets had met. Men
with hot limbs under clothes and men whose bare arms
and legs must have felt cold to the touch, like maple
boughs. Tame men, used to civilization, met glittering
proud men, cool and wild as the Kennebec swans. Men
whose faces, painted like leaves of the autumn, said nothing; nothing more than trees. Men swift and lean and clean
as lynxes, and as silent in their movement, and as full of
bitter, sudden power. It must have been the greatest shock
in the history of the world when these moving maples and
bobcats that went on their hind legs came into contact
with our American ancestors. A shock greater than that of
the Persians on the Greeks. For these men were from different planets, Mercury and Earth.

It was our ancestors' fault that these bobcats leapt
them. From the beginning they had used them like bobcats, like game. The English crowded them out of their

hunting grounds, as they crowded out moose and deer.
English houses and gardens ate away the game lands on
both sides of the Kennebec. This clash of two ideas of land
control was a seed of fire to set the forest in flames. The
French used the Indians like human beings and intermar-
ried with them. The tireless Jesuits, Puritans within the
church to meet the challenge of Puritans outside, walked
into the deepest forest and made Christians of the forest's
children. And the French had them as allies when the battle for the continent began. The forest was on the French
side.

The ancient lords of the Kennebec rose. The Dawn
People sprang to take back the river they had lost. Indians
and French above, English settlers on the lower Kennebec.
The drums began and went on talking up the stream
through the night. Lean men raced like deer on the forest
paths, canoes slid down the river loaded with lynxes that
could paddle, and paddle like the wind.

King Philip was the first spark. He kindled New
England to the south. The flames licked north through the
forest. Saco, Scarborough, Brunswick, New Meadows,
went up in smoke. The flames came right to Merrymeeting
Bay. All Maine west of the river was in ashes. But the English on the east side were unharmed. The Canibas Indians
of the Kennebec were friendly. The eastern Abenakis had
already played with fire and been badly burned. The
Mohawks, whose name was becoming a trans-Atlantic one
like that of the Apache later, friends of the English forever
because the French had once used musket on them, had
come all the way from the Hudson to the Penobscot and
had burned down the Penobscot Indians' villages. The
Penobscot wanted a breathing space. Besides, their chief,
Madockawando, was for peace. And there was a power for
peace  behind him.

That was Baron de Castine, one of the foremost of
Maine's long line of distinguished citizens. This noble lord,
educated in France, an officer in the army at Quebec, had
fallen in love with the forest and the ideal of the simple life
a century before Rousseau. He had gone south and gone
native. To make it complete, he took to himself a dusky

Penobscot princess, daughter of Madockawando, and set up housekeeping. He picked out the finest peninsula in Penobscot Bay, where his name still stands in the midst of loveliness as fresh as on the morning of Creation, and started collecting furs. Very soon he was rolling in furs and clover. Business was good. He amassed 300,000 crowns' worth of the cloths of nature. His lithe and handsome children were soon running the woods in feather and beads. The noble experiment had succeeded and one made by a son of the nation surely the most civilized in Europe. This noble savage also became an American Cicero and his word in the councils was law. He was all for peace and furs.

But the sparks from the west crossed the Kennebec. After King Philip was slain, his men scattered. Some of them came blazing north into Maine. The flames started up again. English traders helped by picking off Indians on the Kennebec and making a pretty penny by selling them as slaves. Five pounds apiece was the price for an Indian scalp current on Monhegan. The Indians did not lay down their arms as ordered. They turned the east bank of the Kennebec into a shambles. The trading post at Woolwich was destroyed. Arrowsic was annihilated; Pemaquid went up in smoke, so did Damariscotta and New Harbor. Monhegan was filled to standing room only with people of the Kennebec empire. The snug houses were gone, the corn was gathered by the crows. The children with yellow curls were gone from the forest.

When peace was made in 1678, some of the men of the empire went straggling back to the river and planted corn again, for their children and for the annual peck the treaty said they must pay to the Indians. The country soon bloomed again. But ten years later, Sir Edmund Andros, James's heavy-handed lieutenant in the New World, could not leave well enough alone. He sent out expeditions to seize the Penobscot country, too. All he succeeded in taking was Baron de Castine's best French furniture and goods. That riled up the baron and he riled up the Indians, who put off the dove and took on the hawk.

The second Indian war began. The Dutch settlement was wiped out and the gardens lay fallow for thirty years.

William and Mary succeeded James II. As usual, there was
war with France. The Indian war borrowed King William's
name for want of a better. Pemaquid was taken once more.
There was blood among the wheat sheaves in Maine,
small boys and women with babe in arms marched behind
Indians, past husbands' and fathers' mutilated bodies, beginning the long trek to Quebec. Again, almost every
house east of Falmouth was a pillar of smoke. Castine's
father-in-law, Madockawando, went far south to find new
wood for his bonfires and burned Dover, New Hampshire.
And Massachusetts swallowed up the smoking ruin of
Maine once more, and for good. The Royal Province of
Massachusetts Bay, it was called, but the western part of it
between the Piscataqua and the Kennebec, claimed by
Massachusetts by purchase from the heirs of Gorges, continued to be known as Maine. East of the Kennebec was
the colony of Sagadahoc.

The first royal governor of Sagadahoc was Sir William
Phips. He was another of the tallest sons of Maine. William
was a broth of a man. His life reads like a Horatio Alger
story. He began eating out of wood and he ended eating
out of silver. He turned to the sea, as did most of Maine's
later great children, to make his fortune. William was born
at Woolwich, east bank of the Kennebec, in 1650. He was
the youngest of twenty-six children, of whom twenty-one
were sons. His father, a gunsmith from Bristol, England,
set the fashion in the size of Maine families. It was a
fashion in my own father's day and it still is among the
newest-come of Maine's fine citizens, the French-
Canadians. While still in his teens, William supported his
mother after the other birds had left the nest and his father
had died. He did it by building ships. He educated himself
when he was resting, at night. Somehow, that seems to be
the best time.

It was lucky that William built ships, for when King
Philip's War broke out, he had a ship to get away in. He
got away, all right, and set himself up as a privateer. He
feathered his floating nest handsomely. He had got wind
of a Spanish treasure ship sunk fifty years before, off the
Bahamas. He got the ear of the Duke of Albemarle, in

London, and breathed the wind into that. The duke fixed
him out for the trip. On his second go, William got the
treasure ship. Thirty-four tons of silver and gold and
pearls—worth about a million and a half dollars. The duke
took most of it, but he generously gave William $70,000
and his wife a cup worth around $400. No one could call
him a stingy lord. King James knighted William and ap-
pointed him High Sheriff of New England. But the posi-
tion was under the hated Andros, and Sir William wasn't
having any. He sailed home and went on privateering. In
1690, he admiraled a great fleet from Boston, the leading
sailor of the New World, and sailed up and captured Port
Royal and all the other Acadian ports. He even took time
off, fifty years before Wolfe, to try and capture Quebec. He
was the first Maine man to try. This thing became a habit.
William missed out in Quebec—his only failure in life. His
failure so set Massachusetts back financially that paper
money appeared for the first time, to stay, sadly enough.

But Sir William helped to rebuild Maine. He built a
fine new fort at Pemaquid and governed his Sagadahoc
splendidly till his death in 1695. He was a man. He had
done a lot in his forty-five years. He had had as many ships
as he had brothers. What became of those brothers is not
known. But I imagine there is much of them in the oak
timbering of my kindred around the Kennebec. His name
is on one of the loveliest villages in all Christendom, on the
lower river, Phippsburg, with its white spire that guided
home the tall ships from China. A man could not want a
whiter or cleaner monument.

King William's War roared on. Phip's spanking fine
fort was cowardly surrendered, the year after Phips died, by
one Chubb, as you might expect from his name. The Peace
of Ryswick did not end the American trouble. But
Madockawando's death did—next year. The Penobscot
were tired and another white-man's disease had decimated
them. They signed the papers at Brunswick, just below
Merrymeeting, on June 7, 1699. The rest of William's
reign, Maine people spent in cleaning up their last witches
and the pirates. Colonel Buck's gravestone was marked
with the foot of the witch he had burned at Bucksport.

Attention was turned to new game. The pirates grew so
bold that they were taking the cod out of Maine fishing
vessels. There was a general roundup. Kidd was caught. He
was probably the scapegoat of greater pirates, some of
them going to church regularly in New York. Anyway, he
made a spectacular end when he and Bradish danced the
hornpipe on nothing in Execution Dock at Plymouth.
But Kidd's soul went marching on. If there is near the
Kennebec's mouth, or elsewhere on the coast, any island
larger than a bushel basket that has not been suggested as a
place where Kidd planted his treasure, I do not know its
name. I own an island that is pockmarked with holes dug
by people looking for it. I have my own first bet. I'll not
say where, but it is near the mouth of my Kennebec. And
the Norway pine sentinel it around, and waves coming
straight from Spain heap the beach below with silver under
the moon. I know where I shall dig. Other people know
things, too: fishermen have told of seeing skulls and diamonds, mixed, ten fathoms down, when the wind is
north-northwest, near Seguin. Others swear they have got
down to doubloons with an auger-like contraption in the
Kennebec marshes, but the treasure keeps going down
deeper. A way treasures have. The best treasure wasn't got
by Kidd, though. Sir William Phips got it. And he, likely,
had more pirate in him than Kidd ever knew about.

  · The accession of Anne, 1702, and the habit of war
with France, started up the third Indian war along the
Kennebec. There had been so many that they stopped
naming them now. Baron de Castine had gone home to
France and philosophy, taking a king's ransom in furs with
him. But his son, a chip off the old block, carried on. He
wanted to be friends with the English, but they wouldn't
let him. They sacked his house and took what he had.
More houses were burned. Blenheim and other European
victories had small counterparts in the New World. By the
Peace of Utrecht in 1713, Acadia, football of France and
England for years, became English forever. The trouble-
some French population was transported to grow up as the
Cajuns of Louisiana and Evangeline started off on her long
search for Gabriel. The Indians signed the peace at

Portsmouth. Saco, Scarborough, Falmouth, Arrowsic, and other villages on the Kennebec were rebuilt. Blockhouses sprang up along the river. The new farms were grouped around a house that could take in the cows and chickens and people at ten minutes' notice. Garrisons replaced trading posts as the chief Kennebec scenery. Fort St. George was built at Brunswick. Georgetown, named for the first of a new batch of kings, was incorporated at the Kennebec's mouth in 1716. The proprietors of the Plymouth Patent built a stone fort at the head of the tide, far up the Kennebec. Sawmills sprang up. Saws sang their hymns of progress and the Indians' teeth were set on edge by the sound. Tall pines fell. The reign of King Log began. York became the shire town of a county now extended to the St. Croix River. The fort at Pemaquid was rebuilt. The Abenakis sulked with burning eyes in the woods, watching all this building. Each hammer blow was aimed at their hearts.

The General Court of Massachusetts offered 150 pounds to any minister who would go down to Brunswick, live at Fort St. George, learn Indian, and bring the Indians into the fold of the redeemed. The Reverend Joseph Baxter of Medfield felt the motion of the spirit. So, after a hundred years without Puritanism, the Kennebec empire got it's first sample. The Indians, though, were beyond redemption. They were already Christians of the Roman Catholic kind. For Father Dreuillettes had been followed by a greater Jesuit, Father Râle, former teacher of Greek in Provence, on the white waters of the Upper Kennebec. There was a fine Roman Catholic church at Norridgewock.

Father Sebastien Râle deserves the name of the third first citizen of Maine. He was French by birth, but the toughness of Maine oak was in him. He had turned Indian for the sake of Indian souls; he was writing a dictionary of Abenaki. He was our first Maine author and he was working on a book of the Indian culture he lived in the midst of. And he loved the lean Abenaki more than life. He had walked thousands of miles through the forest, he had been to the Great Lakes and Illinois, he had learned to live in blizzards, And he had turned half into a bobcat under his black robe. He sat at Norridgewock and turned his bobcat eyes on the tame housecat, Reverend Mr. Baxter of Brunswick, and they had a cold fire in them.

The day of the great endeavor arrived. Governor Dummer of Massachusetts came down to Brunswick on August 9, 1717, and he brought Mr. Baxter and presented him to the Indians. Baxter was to give them the true and Protestant religion, Dummer told the nine sagamores, and if they took Mr. Baxter he would throw in a schoolteacher to teach their children how to read. The Indians looked the gift horse in the mouth. Although they finally permitted the English to build where there had been buildings before, they turned down the Bible and Mr. Baxter. At Norridgewock, Râle smiled.

The Scotch-Irish began to turn Merrymeeting Bay into a continuous farm. Men who had lived for a few generations among the wild and dispossessed Irish kerns found the Indians a brood of sucking doves.

The year 1721 saw the fat in the fire once more. The Indians slew cows and threatened worse things. It was felt that it was time for Mr. Baxter again. He came down. It did not help. Râle and Castine appeared out of nowhere with an army of Abenakis and ordered the English away from the Kennebec. The government's answer was the demand that the Indians give up Râle and all other Jesuits. Any Indian caught with arms was to be seized. Soldiers bagged Castine and took him to Boston. He was finally set free. A price of 500 pounds was set on Râle's head. The black figure stood astride the Kennebec, barring the march of English civilization.

The Reverend Mr. Baxter decided to demolish Râle by theological means. He wrote him a letter. Râle criticized Baxter's Latin; it was not the Latin the Romans used to write. Perhaps the case endings were Protestant or New World ones. Baxter boiled. Father Râle said the English had no right on the Kennebec, it belonged to France. And George I had no right to England, it belonged to the Stuart family. Massachusetts boiled over. Captain Westbrook marched to Norridgewock through the snow of a Kennebec winter. He found the nest, but the bird had

flown. He got Râle's chest with its secret drawer, letters
from the governor of Canada instructing Râle to resist the
English, and Râle's Indian dictionary. He destroyed the
church Râle's red children had built for him. From the
woods, Râle watched the English soldiers marching home
from laying his life in ruins.

An August evening of 1724 saw seventeen whaleboats
moving quietly along the Kennebec below Norridgewock.
It was Harmon of Arrowsic, two hundred soldiers, and
three Mohawks with venom in their eyes, coming from
Fort Richmond. Great Chief Abomazeen, whose name is
kept green on a lovely balsam island called Bomazeen, was
enjoying a peaceful evening's fishing with his wife and
daughter and three sons. The Indian king and queen were
smoking. The salmon were striking well. Then death came
suddenly around the point. Abomazeen and his daughter
leaped into the river—they could swim like salmon—but
there was blood on the ripples where they went down.
Abomazeen's queen was taken alive, biting like a wildcat,
in the arms of a Mohawk. One son lay dead. The other
two escaped.

Father Râle started up from a siesta in his cabin. Hell
was roaring around him. He jumped for his musket. Soldiers were coming around the cabins from two sides,
shooting. The Abenakis went down on their hands and
their faces froze into the silent laughter of death. Some
plunged into the Kennebec, but threw up their arms and
sank under the rain of lead. Father Râles was shot. The
river was open at last to the children of England. The one
man who had straddled it for France and the old church
had finished the fight. It was a half-breed with a French
name, Jacques, who had shot him. Jaquish Island, in
Casco Bay, mostly bare rock and bitter surf, keeps alive the
name of the French half-caste who slew Maine's greatest
missionary.

The fourth Indian war ended with the Treaty of
Falmouth in 1726. The Indians pleaded to have the sale
of firewater to their young men stopped. They asked, too,
to have the fort at Richmond demolished and others that
had been built deep in their lands. They had never signed

any deeds to those places; as long as they could remember, where the forts stood now, there were "Great Long Grown Trees." "God will be angry," they said, "with the man that tells a lie." But the forts remained, new ones crept up deeper into the forest, and the young Indians walked away from the trading posts like men laying nets to catch birds. The young red men did not marry or hunt or fish, they sat around with heads low on their knees and ate the crusts that were thrown to them by the traders. The People of the Dawn bowed their heads to the sunset. The bones of Râle whitened in the Kennebec soil.

The hammers made new music farther and farther up the river. Houses and trading posts shone with their white pine logs and boards. The Huguenots had settled around Richmond, on the west bank. Germans settled Frankfort on the east, giving it an old home name, later changed to Dresden. Scotch-Irish people were marching into new clearings to the tune of bagpipes, driving their cows before them. In 1744, King George stopped playing his harpsichord long enough to flourish his pen and doom a thousand people to death in New England. War between England and France started.

It was men cradled in Maine and the Kennebec Valley that sailed away in 1745 to reduce Louisburg, the Gibraltar of the Western world. Maine lost some of her finest sons, for many settled there, never to return. The smoldering fire burst up and the fifth Indian War began. A price was set on every Indian's scalp—ranging from 100 pounds to a soldier to 400 pounds if the scalper were a private citizen. Every town and hamlet in Maine heard again the old yell that curdled the blood. France offered bounties for English scalps. Bodies of men and women and children lay quiet in fields they would hoe no more. Women awoke to children's screams and babies scalped in the cradle. Cows did not come home and they were found slaughtered, with only their tongues taken. Hate flashed up and down the Kennebec Valley like summer lightning. The river ran streaked with blood. New trails were worn to Quebec and slavery.

They were milestoned with strange agonies. Woe to

the stout captives! Sooner or later they lagged, and then one night there was the fire and the drums and the stiff-legged dances. No wonder the present Yankees of northern New England are lean, lank men. There ancestors lived to come home from Quebec and begat their kind.

The winter of 1747–1748 was the old-fashioned kind, snow six feet on the level. Flour was 10 pounds a hundred-weight. But peace came in 1748. The white settlers crept out into the fields.

But it was only a breathing space. In 1754, the drums were going again, in the forest, in the forts. The sixth and last Indian war was on, with France and England locked in their last grapple for North America. The Maine pines trembled the length of the Kennebec. Horror and death stalked their way along the river for five years.

A little boy looked on and saw his father scalped and mutilated by the Indians, saw them leave the tomahawk sticking up in his skull, and ran home to tell his mother what he had seen. A mother was tending an ailing son when the savages burst in and set a musket to her son's breast. She threw the redskins bodily through a door, lifted the trap door and put the child down cellar. Then she braced against the outside door, holding the Indians out. They shot her through the door. Neighbors found her scalped beside her husband. But the boy was found in the cellar unscratched. A little girl popped into the big oven and lived to tell the story. Another hid in the family churn. A man, scalped, and holding his bowels in his hand, came into a fort and told the people there they would find his silver sleeve buttons where he had hidden them in a stump on his way to fight the Indians. He was given a drink of water and died as he drank.

One Merrymeeting man, surely, stands out as one of the tallest of Maine's sons in the period of Indian warfare. He was Thomas Gyles. He made himself a pretty farm on Pleasant Point. But the Indians came and slew his wife as she was picking her beans in the garden, and Thomas was taken captive. He got way, got himself a new wife and home at Pemaquid, opened up new hayfields, begat a whole quiverful of sons, straightened out the town's

morals, and became chief magistrate of the place. But the
Indians came again, shot him down in his wheat, slew his
men, and captured his wife and children. They let him
kneel down and pray over his sons and then they led him
aside and knocked him in the head. He took it without a
groan, for his children's sake. One son escaped and was
recaptured and burned alive at Castine. Another son, John,
was turned into an Indian for eight years, but he finally
escaped and became the stout commander of the fort at
Brunswick. It was a tough family and it would not be
killed off.

But the end came in 1759. General Wolfe recited his
stanza from Gray's "Elegy" as he rowed across the River of
Death, and next day his scarlet soldiers drove the white-
clad soldiers of France past Wolfe's dying eyes. Quebec was
won and North America was destined to be Anglo-Saxon.
The flames along the Kennebec died down.

In the long bitter century, the first settlers of Maine
had gone back to the days of Homer. Boys of ten had lived
with Hector and Achilles. Gentle women had stood up
over their dead and fought like men. The iron in Maine
men and women was forged in these years. A good deal of
the iron to build a wider nation to the west had been cradled here and tempered in the land of the Kennebec. The
people who were still alive at the close of the Indian wars
were tough people. They could live through anything. The
coming Revolution would be a mere picnic. They had been
tried by the snows of the Maine winters, by ice and
hunger. They had been tried by the Indians. They had
been rocked in a cradle of fire.

Some of the islands in the Kennebec and the bays were
horrible dancing floors. To this day, some islands are
avoided by all living things save the mournful quawks and
herons. The folk memory of the torture islands still lingers.
Fires burned there all night long, long ago.

The Maine men and women weren't the only creatures
built over by the Indian warfare. The dogs grew longer
and keener of ear, too. Many a village was saved by the
barking of dogs. The dogs became artists at reading broken twigs and noticing a far moving shadow. They got so

they could smell Indian a mile away. Probably one of the
most curdling sounds our ancestors ever heard was the
barking of the fort dogs in the depth of the night; and
then the barking was followed by the bubbling-blood yell
in the long Indian throats. Outside and in, the noise was
enough to make the hair stand on end. The Indians grew
to hate the white-man's dog as they hated his master, and
they visited the same tortures upon him. And they took a
wanton delight in butchering livestock on a farm. So the
cows also developed a keen nose for the scent of Indian. A
peaceful cow would swallow her cud, put up her tail, and
tear for the fort. Minutes later, the first scalp lock of horse-
tail hair came into view. Cows were as conscious of the
distance to the fort as their owners. They learned to
browse in sight of it and keep a way open for a sudden return. They grew wise as the Indians, too, in the art of taking cover in the woods. After a raid, it might take weeks to
round up the bossies, still alive, from the forest. There's a
good reason why Maine cows are long of body and lean.
They come of a race that learned how to fit in among
Maine trees and fit in quickly.

Some things the Indians were careful of, though, or
they had learned new superstitions about them. They
scraped the lead from church windows to melt down for
bullets. But they were careful to pile up all the panes of
glass unbroken.

But at last the nights were finished forever when men
fired in the dark at the flash of hostile muskets, the nights
when houses stood lonely in their flames and bodies of
man and wife and child, glistening darkly where their hair
had been, lay sprawled out carelessly and quietly in the
light of the burning home.

Many men left Maine for good in this century of
agony and fire. But the flames that had been their cover-
lets in the cradle of the Kennebec made them tougher
citizen in villages farther west and south, beyond the
Appalachians. So Maine's loss was the nation's gain.

And the oldest natives of all sank down into the dark.
They bowed from sight, as the pines that had brushed the
stars bowed before the sawmills that ate the forest from the

Kennebec's banks. They grew tame and slow and mangy,
sitting with glazed eyes by a campfire without children. Or
they drifted away into the reservations that grew smaller
and smaller as the lusty new natives struck out for more
and more elbowroom. With Quebec fallen, the rock was
gone from under their feet. They had fought hard to keep
the Dawn Land, but they had lost.

A woman who had been a queen came in her rags to
get a dole of grain. It was Christmastime; and the place,
Richmond Fort. The dogs of the post barked at her. One
entry in an old Kennebec journal tells the whole sad tale in
a few words. This queen was blind now, as well as old.

> December 22, 1728
> To the Old blind Squa of abomzeen
> who lay about ye Fort Healpless,
> beging yt ye Governour would
> have marcy on her for
> Christ sake viz. provision.

Those who had fallen fighting were the fortunate ones.
Abomazeen's bones lay in peace at Norridgewock.

At Hallowell, on the river, there is an ancient pine.
When the weather is right, it sends off a blue mist into the
air. People say it is the peace pipe of the Indians smoking
there. Maybe it is. They smoked the pipe and they are
gone forever into peace from the Kennebec.

# 9  Gifts of the Red Gods

One of the greatest errors of history is the impression it constantly leaves of one race's completely supplanting another.

We meet it in history touching on Maine and the rest of America. The French-Indian War ends. The Indians end. As if our Maine ancestors could have lived next-door neighbor to the Abenakis for two hundred years and still have remained European! It is like expecting a book to lie open out in Maine's sunlight and not change color. People who lived with Dawn Men drank in a lot of splendor from them. As if families could eat Indian maize as their chief food for centuries and build their lives about its leaves and silk and geometric loveliness of dried kernels, and still be the same dull eaters of wheat as their race overseas!

The English race finally triumphed over the Indians in Maine. The Indians slowly vanished, but they left the mark of their culture on almost every moment of the colonists' lives.

I should like to set down some of the things we got from the Indians, bright ones and dark ones. Some of them are obvious. Some may come as surprises. We have taken them for granted and have not thought about their origin.

Of course, the Yankees learned how to fight their wars from the Abenakis. They learned to take their color from the forest and to move without making a sound. They learned to creep on their bellies, march Indian file, shoot from behind trees and not expose themselves to the enemy.

The Abenakis taught the Maine farmer how to win the war with winter and the long white hunger. They gave him his wider foot, the snowshoe, the art of banking his house with fir brush, storing his potatoes in earth cellars, drying his apples. The festoons of shriveled beads that hang in farmhouse attics and turn back in water and in the oven into the juicy apples of summer and pies unspeakable are strings of beads the Indians gave us to keep life in our ribs. But they gave us sweeter things. They taught us how to go out into the bare forest and drink the sap of the trees there. They showed us how to notch a tree trunk and catch the sap, and then boil it down into something the Greeks were dreaming about in their ambrosia. To put it into small cakes that carry red manhood in them. Solid heat to carry a man two hundred miles and back through the deepest snow. Take maple sugar off the American table and see what a hole is left.

Well, if it comes to foods, the list will never be done. Take the turkey off our table, take the cranberries, black-berries, huckleberries, the squash, and the Jerusalem arti-chokes. It will be slim pickings after the Indians have taken back their gifts. Nobody can tell me that a man can eat the New World foods and not rise up a New World man. Just as much as the New World weather, our high thunderheads and dazzling sunlight and strong winds, these things be-come a part of a man's thoughts and actions.

But there's a bigger hole yet to be made. Take away the vegetable that has built the square corners of our Yan-kee chins and heads—take away the Indian corn. You might as well remove the table. Our forefathers learned how to soak the skin off these nuggets of life, steam them, turn maple sugar over them, and then sit down smack on the banks and braes of Beulah Land. Hulled corn is only one feast brought to us by the Indian god in green. Corn parched, corn steamed on the cob, corn ground into meal and baked, boiled, fried, and hot, cold, and neuter. The sinews of the pioneer and the Declaration of Independence were built out of hasty pudding. You can slice it and fry it next morning. You can bring up a family of twenty-one sons on it. You can eat it striped with molasses as dessert, or you can eat it as roast, salted down with great slabs of dried cod. You can stir the meal into the Kennebec

Dundee pudding—named by the Kennebec Scotch-Irish—
and throw every sweet and substantial thing in the house
into it as it seethes; raisins, citron, pork scraps, whisky if
you have it, and faith. You roll Kennebec smelts in this
meal that is America and they come out of the oven in
strips of the pavements of Jerusalem the Golden. Of
course, there's johnnycake left. That alone could have produced Israel Putnam, the minute men, and the long, lean
men taking their big families west. No Maine housewife
could get along without corn meal; her whole household
would   collapse.

The Abenakis taught the Kennebec men how to raise
the maize. A mound of earth between the stumps, three or
four kernels, and a fat alewife to each hill, method was necessary in Maine as it was hard to find more than that much
space free of stumps, rock, junipers, or woodchucks. Maine
gardens are spot gardens, you hang them on the hillside
as best you can. If there is a finer or lovelier symbol of a
nation's strength than an ear full of kernels seen through
the split in a cornhusk, I don't know it. As a design, it
beats the acanthus leaf all hollow.

The Kennebec Indians taught us to eat out of doors
and keep things warm at the same time. That was no les-
son to be sneezed at. They taught us how to take common
rockweed, a common fire and common clams, roll them all
together, and sit down for a few minutes and let nature
take her course. Then all you have to do is turn back the
top rockweed and discover a banquet that makes a man as
full of ginger as a god.

They taught us the whole art of trapping, of course,
and how to skin animals, tan pelts, and wear fur clothes.
They taught my father how to build a fire on a ledge in a
Maine pasture, then sweep the ashes off and roll up in a
blanket on it, and sleep warm all a March night. I want to
thank them personally for that. I should never have got to
know the March stars if it hadn't been for the Abenakis.
They showed us how to turn the fragile bark of the birch
into canoes. They schooled us in almost all that we know
about hunting moose, deer, ducks, geese, and smaller
game. They even gave us decoys and the moose horn.

They showed us the way to stalk game and how to read the hieroglyphics of a snowy morning and know what meats we shall have for dinner. If we as a nation are an outdoor one, if the summer vacation, the camping trip, the hunting and fishing trips, are institutions of American life, then to the Indians be the glory for these things that are the salt of our lives.

Behind all these features of our life that we take so for granted is a splendid and mysterious fact. Those slim men, so close cousins to the birch trees and the dawn stars and the wind, helped our grandfathers and great-grandfathers to return to the boyhood of the human race, to go back to the tents of Isaac and Jacob, the greenwood of Robin Hood and Maid Marian, to the saga cycle of life of the Scottish Border. They took us back to ancient strengths, when a man's life was in his two arms, to a man's starting out with only one tool and building security for himself in the forest, back to years when a man's strength was duty and his begetting sons an act of God. The Indians helped us to strip off the clothes of Europe that were poisoning and stifling us and bathe in the sunlight and the starlight, in the splendor of autumn woods. They taught us to be boys again and plunge in the fountains of youth that sparkle under blue skies and glittering evergreens. One of the early Kennebec chiefs was called Robin Hood by the colonists. Our fathers knew what a glory they were living in. Without the Indians to blaze the trails, there would have been no pioneers.

There's a lot of American psychology you can explain only by the fact that we went Indian for a time.

When little Kennebec boys get so full of spring that they can't hold it in any longer, and bend in their chins and let out a high-pitched liquid call deep in their throats that carries to their playmates three farms away, they are paying a slender, bright tribute to the Indians of long ago. For that New World yodeling of theirs is the Indian war cry, kept alive by American boys, and a secret even they lose when they become men. The Dawn People are calling across April from centuries ago.

The Indians led our forefathers to the spruce trees, put

the pungent spruce resin into their mouths, and so started the movement that went over the continent like a vast ripple and set a million jaws to working. There's no sense in my more than mentioning the word tobacco. It tops even maize as the Indians' gift to the universe. Sir Walter Raleigh's last act in a life crowded with them was to take a pipe of tobacco, to settle his spirits before the ax fell. It is the noblest preparation for death. And the best pipe to smoke it in is the pipe that brings two golden Indian gifts together, the Kennebec corncob.

If the Abenakis had taught us nothing more than how to make bayberry candles, that would entitle them to wear a halo.

When I was a boy and full of the Old Boy bigger than a woodchuck, as my aunt would put it, my mother and aunts would call me by a name that once was commonly used on all Kennebec boys.

"Come here, you little sannup!"

That word is the Abenaki one for warrior, for the male Indian. My elders did not know how right they were in calling me a young savage. They were using a word folk-consciously and, so, unconsciously. But they were doing more. They were saying that their ancestors and mine had lived for three centuries side by side with Abenakis, learning from them how to live up to a Maine winter, how to live up to the "bright bees of a Kennebec snowstorm," how to live up to a birch tree in blossom, or the tall maize with its golden hair flowing in the sunlight of a Maine September day. They were saying plainly that the Indians had taught them how to be good Americans.

# 10  A Man of Principle

The first men on the Kennebec were not churchly
men. They were after fish and furs and farms. They had a
lot of juice in them. They sang merry songs and kicked up
their heels in the dance. Some of the later comers were ex-
iles for religion's sake, the Huguenots of Richmond and
the German Moravians of Dresden. But they were not men
who took their religion like a knife in their ribs. And they
were leavened by Irish and Scotch and Scotch-Irish and
Anglican Englishmen. Puritan stock came in at last, but
Puritans were not a majority. By 1750, there was a pretty
good cross section of all the Colonial religions on the
Kennebec: Anglicans, Catholics, Calvinists, Lutherans,
Moravians, Independents, and just plain nothing. They
got on together without cutting one another's throats.
From the beginning, the Kennebec was the freest river in
America, a river of toleration, a live-and-let-live river.

So when the old battle of Whig and Tory transferred
itself to the forests of North America and the Revolution
was in the air, it was natural that there should be so many
Tories living along the Kennebec. The best families, the
ones in the big houses, were for the king; the Gardiners
and Richards' of Gardinerstown, the Vaughans of Hallowell, the Dumaresqs of Swan Island. They were solid, substantial citizens, and the Whiggish element was often made
up of the footloose and the newcomers. Though they were
conservatives in politics, these river princes were liberal
men in the issues of life in general. They did not condemn
mince pies or Christmas greens as ungodly. It was John
Gardiner of Gardinerstown who spoke for the theater in
the Massachusetts Assembly, later on, against the narrow

Puritanic minds. The Province of Maine was always a
strange and unwilling bedfellow of the Puritan state.
When the patriots of Boston went Indian on tea and
Continental on government, the Loyalists of the Kennebec
stood by the old principles. Dr. Sylvester Gardiner called
Washington, the father-to-be of his country, a thief. And
Benedict Arnold stole his nails for his trouble, when he was
going by that way and needed nails for his boats. There is a
local tradition that I have come upon, that people in Revo-
lutionary times were able to recognize the Tory places
along the Kennebec by the Lombardy poplars. Maybe it
was so. For the Tories would have been the ones interested
in fine gardens and fine trees.

There was, as Maine people say, the devil to pay and
no pitch hot when the storm finally burst. One of the most
brilliant of the Continental Congress's campaigns went
right up the Kennebec, through the Tory country. And
there was fur flying in Maine towns, little houses against
big houses, liberty poles going up and widows crashing in,
and tar boiling over and bedticks shaking out their feathers
for a New World holiday.

And there was one king's man who stood up by the
Kennebec and would not pull in his horns. He was the
fourth of Maine's tallest sons and our second author,
Parson Jacob Bailey, the Frontier Missionary.

Bailey was a Harvard man, in John Adams's class,
though at the foot, for his poverty's sake, in Harvard's
caste system. He had taught school in Massachusetts, after
taking orders in England, and had not liked it. So he
joined the Society for Propagating the Gospel in Foreign
Parts, and came down to the Kennebec to put the fear of
God and the Anglican creed in the heathen there, in 1760.

The parson found a lot of heathenish things. Boys
going barefoot and men going it like boys, a lot of free-
and-easy habits as regards wives, and worst of all, profanity.
Jacob could stand anything but that. He lifted his skirts
and sailed in. There was no church on the Kennebec, not
east of Brunswick. There were a lot of different religions,
but they were not Anglican and did not count. Bailey
picked out Pownalborough, county seat of the newly

created Lincoln County, as his place. He stayed with
Captain Goodwin until a parsonage was built for him. He
pounced on the new Pownalborough courthouse the
minute it was built, and used it for his church. It was a fine
three-decker courthouse, the court below, the judge's family above, and the soldiers barracked on top to hold them
all down. John Adams tried a case there and later on Dan
Webster came there twice to plead.

The parson got him a wife, started Anglican services
everywhere, at Harpswell, Georgetown, Richmond, Falmouth, going through snow six feet deep in winter to
spread the light among a half dozen different flocks. He
baptized babies and fathers who had missed baptism. He
walked the banks of the Kennebec on both sides, hundreds
of miles each year. He fired the Gardiner family to build
him his church, St. John's, in Pownalborough, in 1770,
and another at Gardinerstown, nine miles upriver. He was
everywhere, worked night and day, started a family of children, a garden that was probably one of the best in North
America, commenced his journal, began archeological in-
quiries into Indian mounds, wrote his history of the Kennebec country, cultivated the muse in good rolling eighteenth-century verses, and he did it all on no salary at all.
He was a militant agriculturist. He admired good potatoes.
The Kennebec soil was fine for them. He writes that it
could produce eight hundred bushels an acre. Merrymeeting spread out blue below his windows, with the
White Mountains behind; wild flowers he had tamed, arbu-
tus and trilliums, unrolled before his doorstep. Life was
good. The wilderness was blossoming like the rose.

But there were worms in his rose. Not all the bigwigs
around were Anglicans. They began to make things hot
for the parson. One of them claimed the land on which
his parsonage stood. Judge Bowman was a very big worm
in the rose. The south wind brought hot waves of the
Colonial wrath around Boston. The Kennebec, as well as
Boston Harbor, had its tea party, and barrels of the "ac-
cursed weed" were dumped out for the benefit of the surprised salmon of Merrymeeting Bay. Parson Bailey did not
keep quiet about that. He had a genius for not keeping

quiet about anything. He said it was a queer kind of sacred
liberty that had to vent its wrath on innocent tea. He said
a great deal more before long. He peppered his journal
with strong words. He had lived so long in the midst of
profanity that he had gotten the habit. He went out of his
way to rile up the "sons of liberty." He sprinkled the
cayenne of his sarcasm up and down the Kennebec. Mobs
were going about nightly, smelling out tea in haymows and
loyalty to George III. Householders had to buy them off
with rum. Parson Bailey didn't. He told them what he
thought of liberty and sedition and imbecility. He refused
to take the covenant and he forbade his people to do so.
He loved George III and to hell with traitors. So the yells
of mobs rang around the parsonage. Coming back on foot
from Boston, in 1774, the parson was mobbed at
Brunswick and he had to go into hiding for two days. A
hundred armed sons of liberty hunted for him, headed by
patriotism and strong liquor. They finally got to fighting
among themselves and forgot Bailey. When the wind blew
up from Lexington, the parson was "assaulted by ruffians."
Commotions and committees kept him in hot water all
summer. A Tory relative was prevented from landing his
goods and family. A mob surrounded Bailey's house and a
man named Harvey aimed his loaded musket at the parsonage windows, where the parson's children were looking
out round-eyed. Harvey yelled out, according to the parson, "This is a damned nest of damned Tories, and I'm
going to blow as many of them to the devil as possible!"
He snapped his gun several times, but it would not fire.
Providence was on the parson's side and put the spark out
each time. A few minutes later, at the courthouse, the gun
went off beautifully. A miracle, and nothing less!

The militant preacher went out of his way to paint por-
traits of the sons of liberty. One of these "angels from
heaven" on the Kennebec, named Whiting, had been
kicked first out of Harvard, said Bailey, and then out of the
college at Providence, for stealing the president's horse.
This horse thief had set himself up as a schoolmaster on
the Kennebec and as a preacher against the Anglican
Church. Another angel of light, Alden, was an Anabaptist,

or worse, from England. He had been kicked, too. He had been unfrocked twice for immorality, tried at the Old Bailey for perjury, immorality, and general depravity. Now he was a preacher on the Kennebec.

The woods were full of Anabaptists, Brownists, Presbyterians, and Massachusetts narrowheads drawing the parson's flocks from the fold. Good Anglicans were being taxed and a Congregational church was going up in the midst of acres the parson had cleared of weeds and heathenism. It was not to be borne. The parson rolled up his sleeves in the pulpit.

He had the good sense to leave home, though, when Arnold was preparing his bateaux under the parsonage windows. Other Loyalists took a vacation at this time, and shuttered their windows. Parson Bailey did, too. It was all right to fight a mob of a few hundred men; an army of a thousand was too many. But he was at home off and on, and later he wrote an account of Arnold's brilliant failure. He applauded when the Indian allies from Norridgewock deserted and went back to the freedom of the forest and left the freedom of the Continental Congress kind in the lurch.

Once Arnold was gone, Bailey came out in his old glory. There was a famous hubbub at Christmastime. New Year's Day, the young bloods raised a liberty pole and went Indian. They drank and swore and yelled out imprecations, said Bailey, like the traitors they were. Some of them were all for dragging Bailey out and making him consecrate the pole. Somebody thought better of it and so the Pownalborough green was saved from being a shambles, maybe, the New Year's Day, 1776. For the parson was hopping, hopping mad; and he had blood in his eye. Next morning there was bedlam, for the sacred pole had been chopped down. Everybody swore Bailey did it. He had cut at the root of American independence. The hue and cry was raised. The parson had to write a letter denying that he had swung the ax on it. The parson let himself go in the letter. He was sorry the sons of liberty had lost their idol. He was sorry the pole was cut down. Better a thousand poles instead of one if simple-minded people got any pleasure from them. They were all a parcel of damned fools. "You are sensible," the parson wrote, "that liberty may subsist without any pole at all; and if all the pines, spruces, and fir were lying prone upon the ground, it would not elevate tyranny a bit." It was small wonder the heathen worshiped idols, when Kennebec Christians bowed down before a Kennebec spruce. What a place for liberty Maine was with all its millions of balsams!

All the same, I suspect the parson did cut the thing down. In the heat of New Year festivity, probably.

Parson Bailey got out of that tight corner. But disasters followed fast thereafter, in the first year of American independence. Half his flock left his church. Curses followed him on the street. He was named a mortal enemy of his country for not keeping the thanksgiving decreed by the Continental Congress. His flower garden was trampled. Presbyterians killed seven of his twelve sheep and shot his best heifer. He was haled before committees, put under bonds, forbidden to include the king in his prayers. But Bailey set his Anglican jaw and dug his heels into the ground. When the Declaration of Independence came out, he refused to read it from the pulpit. He went right on praying for the king. Some whole weeks he had to hide away in his house. Sometimes things got so hot that he had to leave his wife and children and take refuge in Boston, among secret sympathizers with the king. He was coming back from such a flight when he heard, at Portsmouth, the melancholy news of the Yankee victory at Saratoga. He had to flit like a ghost in the night. Tories in Boston helped keep him alive. His congregation dwindled. He was finally locked out of his church. He fought to the end. But the odds were too great. He gave up at last and asked the Massachusetts General Court for permission to remove to Halifax. He got the permission. But there were delays. And the day before Christmas he made a last gesture of defiance and held services in his old church. He said that Anabaptists, "Separates," Quakers, and convicts were not forced to take the oath, why should he be obliged to? He had a visit from the high sheriff on Christmas Day.

The time came at last, in June 1779, when he was allowed to leave the beautiful valley that he had filled with the worship of God, and better seed potatoes, better apple trees, and flowers from overseas. The labor of a lifetime was lost. A war had ruined it all. He sat down to pen his farewell to the Kennebec. "Must we leave these pleasing scenes of nature," he wrote with a fine eighteenth-century flourish to his pen, "these friendly shades, these rising plants, these opening flowers, these trees swelling with fruit, and yonder winding river, which appears through the umbrageous avenue, to revive and elevate the mind: We must no longer behold the splendid orb of the day peeping over the eastern hills to dissipate the fog, and to brighten the field and forest. We must hear no more the sweet music of the tuneful tribe, amidst the trembling grove, to gladden, charm, and animate the desponding heart."

It was hard to go. There was a small grave, too, among the improved apple trees. He would never see that again, either. Good-bye, Maine spruces and birches, Maine thrushes, and sunrise like a forest fire along the Kennebec, and his child's mound. Prose was not fine enough. He must say it in a purer medium. He swung into verse. Good-bye to his flowers:

> No more for me the lovely rose
> Her open blushing charms disclose,
>     Nor breathes her rich perfume;
> I now renounce my boasted skill
> To plant the snowy daffodil
>     Nor teach her where to bloom.

Goodbye, Kennebec spring and Kennebec fall:

> In pensive thought I often rove
> Thro' the tall forest and the grove,
>     Where vernal beauties rise;
> And when the summer's charms decay
> I then your trembling leaves survey
>     Stain'd with autumnal dyes.

Good-bye Kennebec River:

Ye verdant banks of Kennebec,
Which numerous plants and flowers bedeck,
   Thou great majestick stream,
To swell whose silent, sullen tide
A thousand lesser rivers glide,
   No more my favorite theme.

The Kennebec had lost its first poet.

A few friends came to see him off. He had saved a few things and got them aboard the boat. He had his bedstead and about forty dollars worth of other furniture. The boat was at the garden's end. He went aboard. He got on a ship at Georgetown. He sailed off to the land of exile, Nova Scotia. He had fought a good fight and kept the faith.

Bailey was given a berth as chaplain to a British regiment in Halifax. The old soldier in him must have enjoyed that. He got on in exile. He lived to see his children prosper. But his heart was left on the altar of St. John's at Pownalborough and among his apple trees by the blue Kennebec.

Parson Bailey admired Father Râle, that earlier centurion of the Lord, who had also been driven from his church. Into the grave, not into the land of exile. It was the same. Râle had been mistaken in his religion, being a Roman Catholic, but Bailey admired an honest zeal. Trust one good soldier to know another when he saw him.

# 11  Benedict Arnold's March to Quebec

There has been a lot of hard marching in history. Xenophon and the ten thousand Greeks did some, and so did Napoleon's Grand Army coming home through a Russian winter. David Ingram did a smart bit of walking along the whole seacoast of North America, without any white man to talk with. But for downright mean going, fit to wear a man right down to withing, as Cap'n Bibber would say, that march takes the cake which Arnold made up the Kennebec in 1775, to storm Quebec.

Though Washington gave the order, it was probably Arnold's brilliant idea, this plan to capture Quebec by way of Maine. It was good theater and Arnold always had a gift for that. Anyway, Colonel Arnold got his orders and an army of eleven hundred men. It was an army to warm the cockles of a colonel's heart. It was made up of equal parts solid farmer stock and wildcats. There were a great many Scotch-Irish in it. The American Revolution would have been no revolution worth talking about if it hadn't been for the Irish, men whose fathers and grandfathers had seen Belfast's great industries ruined and had brought energy and a terrible hatred against England overseas with them to seed American fields. There was a son of Erin at every campfire to keep the war going by sheer wit and oratory. But Arnold had, too, a lot of Pennsylvania Dutchmen, built close to the ground and made solid by good cookery and childlike faith in a solid Moravian God. Hardheaded Yankees of Massachusetts, Rhode Island, and Connecticut were thrown in to add toughness. And to leaven the whole, there were a lot of rakish demigods from the Old Dominion, able to lick their weight in lynxes three times a day. The army had a leader, stout and florid and reckless enough to go ahead of them all into Tophet, not strong on bookkeeping or rations, but a man good at covering ground and being a god men could worship. There were a lot of future statesmen and scalawags and future authors in the army. Aaron Burr was there. John Joseph Henry, a Scotch-Irish youth who had run away from home in Pennsylvania, was there and was shocked at the language used by his fellow soldiers. He wrote about the expedition. So did half a dozen others. The men had rather surprising uniforms, gray hunting shirts, all over fringes, and long leggings. They looked more like Indians than the Indians themselves. Some of the men had shoes, but they carried them carefully in their hands, to save them, and went in moccasins. Everybody had a gorgeous hat. Some hats had patriotic mottoes. John Henry had a feather in his. The men were armed with a rifle-barreled gun, a tomahawk, an ax, a nice knife for scalping, about a foot long, and a confidence in God and in the strength and courage of their own high hearts.

They started out from Cambridge, footed it to Newburyport, and took ship on eleven schooners on September 18th. A few of the lukewarmer patriots had to have guard to keep them from leaving the ships before they got under way. They made the Kennebec's mouth by midnight. Here they shipped pilots. Arnold hove to six hours in Parker's Flats; and the Reverend Mr. Parker of Bath came out and prayed an hour and a half over Captain Dan Morgan's Virginia riflemen. Having enlisted the Deity on the side of the Old Dominion, the Virginians sailed on. Sam McCobb, of Georgetown, a delegate of the Provincial Congress, was there waiting to join up. He had marched his company of Kennebeckers to Boston in six days to fight behind the rail fence at Bunker Hill; then, hearing of Arnold's trip, he ran his men back home again, got twenty recruits, and came aboard. Now that Maine was represented, the expedition could go on.

The army sailed under the windows of the Pownalborough courthouse, where Major Goodwin, surveyor of the
Plymouth Company, lived, passed Parson Bailey's empty
nest, up the channel east of Swan Island, and landed at
Pittston. Arnold put up at Major Colburn's. The major
had been building two hundred bateaux on order for
Arnold. He had them ready. Each would carry six or seven
men. They were propelled by four paddles and two poles.
They were made of pine, ribbed with oak. But the pine was
green, and the "crazy things" were a great disappointment
to the men later on. They were heavy as sin to tote and
they went to pieces with astounding ease. Major Colburn
came along with his boats. Everybody cursed them. But it
was looking a gift horse in the mouth, for the major never
got a red cent for building them and his family later on
petitioned Congress for years without luck. At Pittston,
the army gathered provisions: five hundred bushels of
corn, salt, pork, flour, and sixty barrels of salt beef. They
left the ships and took to the bateaux.

They were at Fort Western, September 23rd. Arnold
lay at Captain Howard's. A vast barbecue was given in his
honor. Jacataqua, the queen of Swan Island, was there, and
she and the other womenfolk who were to go were
shipped, and the dogs. Almost everybody had a dog. They
saved lots of patriots' lives later, these walking soup
kitchens. The order of march was discussed. It developed
that Dan Morgan of Virginia, though junior to almost
everybody, would not go unless he could lead. Dan was a
born leader. He stood six-feet-four in his moccasins and
wore on his hat in letters of gold "Liberty or Death." He
was as hot-tempered as a kettle of fat, a Spartan for disci-
pline and decorum, and he looked and walked like a Greek
god. His Virginians were hickory and iron. "They were
beautiful men," wrote John Henry, "who know how to
handle a rifle." So Arnold humored him and Daniel led the
van. The army set off in four divisions, by foot and paddle
and elbow grease up the river. Farmers with oxen turned
out and dragged the bateaux around the first falls. Arnold
watched them go past, with glory in his eyes. A scout pa-
trol was sent ahead to blaze the way to the Chaudiere

River. Arnold waited till most of the army was off, then he
darted ahead in his birch canoe to overtake Dan Morgan.

At the ruins of Fort Halifax, near today's Waterville,
the men had a chance to heft the bateaux. They carried
them on four handspikes, four men to each, around the
falls. They packed the hundred tons of provisions on their
backs. This story was repeated every so often, for the upper
Kennebec is full of falls. At the Five Mile Rips, the bateaux
started leaking. There were houses still, almost the last
white outpost, and a fearful gorge above, where the
bateaux were paddled uphill with men helping with ropes
from the cliffs. The first ice came, "a pain glass thick," and
the men's clothes froze stiff. The soldiers sweat blood here.
Bombazee Rips next, then the ruins of old Norridgewock,
and Râle's grave marked with a cross. A few cabins and a
baby fourteen months old! Then the Great Falls of Norridgewock, a descent of ninety feet by the river in one mile.
Some oxen were still available to drag supplies overland.
But the men sweat still more blood and their arms
wrenched at the shoulder sockets till they burned like fire.
A huge rock stood mournful in the dizzy water, eaten away
by Indians seeking arrowheads for thousands of years.
Arnold stayed here from October 2nd to 9th, waiting for
his third and fourth divisions. Now the provisions went
bad wholesale. Rain unsalted the salt fish, the bread
molded, the peas spoiled, the salt beef, put up in hot
weather, was discovered to be carrion. Only the flour and
the pork were left. Rations were shortened. The men ate
the oxen as they caved in under the yoke. Somebody
brought down a moose. Others caught trout. There were
juicy tidbits of fat beaver tails.

The army carried around Carratunk Falls, popularly
called Hell Gate. The last pioneer cabins, the last rough
roads—goodbye civilization! They entered the gateway
into the mountains here. The wilderness closed dark upon
them. The gloom of the high spruces came down like a
vast shadow over the men's minds and all the splendor
went out of the expedition.

Even today you can spot the way they went, for they
cut a swath through the evergreen forest and hardwood

came up where they had passed. That swath followed up
the west branch of the Kennebec, the Dead River. But to
avoid the rapids of the junction, the army had to cut their
way across country, by a chain of forest lakes. Where the
scouts had blazed trees, a road was made through spruces
and cedars a foot thick and standing so close a deer might
not slip through. Many axes had been left behind, so men
had to use tomahawks and knives on the forest giants.
They had to carry all their goods, seven or eight trips for
each man, eight or nine miles. Rain came, and snow, and
the first casualty—a soldier smashed by a falling tree.
Equipment was abandoned, chests of balls, guns, spoiled
food. A century later bateaux were found in the bogs here;
seasoned sound at last where tired men dropped them. The
army crawled up a mile or two of hell. Then a pond. Then
a swamp, and cedar roots that cut to the bone as the men
stumbled knee-deep. Another pond. Then three miles
more of morass. Down the mountain. The last mile was a
"savanna," with "elegant green moss." It looked lovely
going. And when the soldiers got into it, it sucked them
down to the waist, and snags of dead trees cut their feet
and legs like so many razors. There are bogs and bogs, but
none to equal a Kennebec spruce swamp. Whoever has
walked in one will find the hot asphalt of Tophet a pleasant
lawn. More snow. Ice to cut above the snags. Sickness
came, diarrhea, dysentery, pneumonia. The forest was full
of sick men. A log hospital went up, those strong enough
to walk started home, boats were left at the ponds to ferry
them over. The army was two armies now, one going
north, one south.

The scouts sent ahead to find a way to the Chaudiere
returned. Or rather, the army overtook them crawling or
sitting on stumps, unable to move. They had done their
work, blazed the trail, and seen the river. But they were
skeletons, not men. They would never have come back if it
hadn't been for one man. Maine did not have many soldiers in this army, but it supplied Jeremiah Getchell. If it
hadn't been for him, there would have been no army
storming Quebec. He was a Kennebec man, one of the
regular kind, another tall son of Maine. Jeremiah led the

scouts up the Dead River and back. John Henry was
among them. He sang Jeremiah's praises. This native had
never been up the Dead River, but he had the Maine grit
to go. He was "sheer wisdom," Henry says, wise as the Indians in the ways of the forest. He had a compass between
his ears and cedar inside his leather breeches. But he was a
Maine man in being full of the good salt of humor, too.
He made the men laugh. The day when they were traveling a lake so deep in mountains that perpetual twilight
came over them, Jeremiah looked at young John Henry's
woeful face. "Johnny," said he, "you look like a dark-blue
leather whetstone!" And Johnny had to smile and go on
paddling. Getchell taught them how to use fir boughs to
make beds that were like mattresses from heaven every
night, even in the snow. When food ran short, Getchell
showed them how to get a cordial out of trees. He cut a
gash under the blisters on the firs, pressed his knife above,
and filled his mouth with pungent sap more heartening
than brandy, a wine of the sun.

They passed the horror of lost lakes and forests at the
God-forsaken height of land. One day an Irishman of the
party, named Cunningham, climbed a lofty pine and saw
the winding Chaudiere, the roadway down to the St.
Lawrence, and the smoke of a faraway French settlement.
The party turned back. They went on wind-pudding now.
But Getchell kept the life in them, and a dash of humor.
John Henry noticed him covering up all their tracks as he
ran last behind them, obliterating the trail and keeping up
with them at the same time. At night he made them a pork
broth out of their last bits of pork, each man holding his
hunk on a stick and taking it out when the broth was
done. He mended their canoe with new rolls of birch, fir
pitch, pork grease, and the roots of cedar trees. They got a
moose; Getchell split the bones for the marrow, they were
starving for want of fat. Back down the Dead River the
Kennebec Odysseus led his men. Their knees gave out at
last. Morgan found them where they had fallen. Morgan
was a sight for sore eyes. He was going now with thighs
bare and only an Indian loincloth, and his skin was lacer-
ated with scars from Maine spruces. John Henry rejoined

his Pennsylvania Dutchmen and made short work of the pork and dumplings set before him.

The whole army moved up along the scouts' trail. The Dead River looked easy, but they found it swift and too deep for the poles. They pulled along by bushes on the banks. The river boxed the compass every so often; they paddled sixteen miles to cover eight as the crow flies. Rations were halved. The weaker men were sent back. On October 19th, the rain began in earnest, days of it. The river rose eight feet in one night. The soldiers awoke in floating tents. John Henry took a long ride under the Dead River when his bateau upset. "We are going to heaven!" he cried as he went down. He saw his friend Simpson's gold-laced hat above the water. Henry was saved by one of the many Irishmen. He was too modest to take off his leather breeches, but his comrades peeled them off him and dried them by the fire. But the breeks went hard on him, he had to rub them half the night, with the stars beholding his  immodesty. His hat was gone, and the feather, but he got another hat from a sick soldier and could go on to war. Simpson was saved, too, and he sang "Plato," sitting on a stump. It became the whole army's song. Many boats were lost. Many men had to walk, trees were felled for bridges. Savage cold set in. The weaklings were weeded out again. It snowed. Boats capsized. Provisions, ammunition, and money were lost. Some soldiers tried making soup of rawhide. Some had only their candles to eat. Arnold hurried ahead to reach food in Canada. Something like mutiny burst forth as his shadow melted into the forest. On October 25th, Captain Enos turned back with nearly one-third of the dwindling army. McCobb went, too, forgetting Bunker Hill. The deserters took more than their share of provisions. Enos was later court-martialed at Cambridge, but was acquitted. This defection probably cost the Colonies Canada.

Arnold, still living on hopes and not much more, threaded his way somehow through the maze of the height of land, through whole forests blown down, bogs, lakes, savage ravines. He got to Megantic Lake. The rest—the six hundred of them—came after, over "The Terrible Carrying

Place." The Virginians were outpaced at last by the
tougher Dutchmen. But Morgan insisted on taking his
bateaux where the others had dropped theirs. His men
wore their shoulders through to the bone. John Henry saw
the exposed shoulder blades. There was deep snow. Many
of the men were barefooted now, even the rags they had
tied over their naked soles were worn away. They marched
in freezing water to their middles. A nearsighted drummer
kept falling off all the logs and was the laughingstock of
the whole army. But he got to Quebec with his precious
drum, where stronger men had died.

    Jacquin, one of the scouts sent ahead, came back with
news that the French habitants were eager to assist the
Americans. The army started down the Chaudiere and
walked into a terrible trap of marshland. The ice gave
under them and they had to wade waist-deep. John Henry
thought he knew more than the leader. He chose a new
path and sank to his armpits. Sergeant Grier's wife upped
her skirt above her waist and led the men on. She was a
big woman. John Henry blushed. Another wife, Mrs.
Warner, hearing her husband had been abandoned sick in
the forest, went back in tears to stay with him. The
Chaudiere was a cauldron, like its name. The last bateau
was stove into kindling. Arnold went under, but swam
ashore. Most of the guns were lost. All food was gone.
Men ate dog meat, the uppers of their shoes, their car-
tridge boxes. They dug in the sand for roots and fought
over them. Many were left to turn into bleaching skeletons
in the woods there. John Henry came upon a group of
men and threw himself, exhausted, on a log by their fire;
his weight upset two-thirds of the soup they were cooking,
and a man sprang up and pointed his gun at him. But John
Henry did not move. He would have welcomed death. By
and by, the men made friends with him and gave him a cup
of the soup. They said it was bear. It looked dark green.
John Henry took one taste and that was enough. It was
the black Newfoundland dog John had seen with these
troops. He meditated suicide. Then along came Simpson
and saved him by singing "Plato." It wasn't Handel, as
John Henry wrote, but it saved his life. They all chewed

boiled leather for supper.

Arnold got to the French and sent back cattle to his starving troops. John Henry's Captain Smith heard the lowing and the faint huzzas of the weakened men. In a burst of generosity, he gave John Henry his whole dirty strip of bacon and John Henry swallowed it all in one gulp.

John first saw Aaron Burr here, handsome still after the march. He went on to the slaughter place, to the "Abyssinian feast." The men devoured the cattle half raw. John watched a man downing a whole colon of an ox. One big Pennsylvania Dutchman ate himself to death. John Henry ate slowly and sparingly, being wise. The French peasents were amazed to see men who had come through such a hell. The report spread that the Americans, dressed in armor, had emerged from the forest. The skin of the Americans was darker than rusty armor and as hard as iron. It had to be to last. So half of the army came out of the shadow of the forest, five hundred of the thousand who had gone in, five hundred skeletons out of Tophet.

The rest was anticlimactic; the real campaign was over and Arnold had won it. The army moved on through Canuck farmlands and reached Ste. Marie by Novmber 5th. Arnold took M. Tashereau's house for headquarters. His host was not at home, he had gone to Quebec, to which place all the French had been ordered by the British on pain of having their roofs burned over them. The Americans drank his wine and ate his turkeys. What was left of the army was reorganized. All the men got moccasins. John Henry fell sick from eating too much beefsteak. Arnold put him to bed in a French home and gave the people $2 for his keep. John lay in the heart of the house, by the stove, and the red-cheeked family revolved around him in homespun. They got him on his feet and even found him a boat to take him downriver. They would not take the $2.

The Americans reached the St. Lawrence, only to find all the boats gone from their side and two British men-of-war patrolling the river. But Arnold took his tattered army across the water, right under the noses of the frigate

*Lizard* and the sloop *Hunter*, and the British guard boats
going back and forth, on an "exceeding dark night." They
landed at Wolfe's Cove and climbed by his path to the
Plains of Abraham. The wind came up and the moon burst
from the clouds, and they could not go back a fourth time
to fetch the scaling ladders. There they were, three hundred fifty men, bent on capturing the strongest citadel in
North America. Arnold marched right up to the walls. The
Quebec soldiers and citizens came out on the ramparts.
They gave the Americans a cheer! The Americans cheered
back. Then some spoilsport Continental ended it all by
starting to shoot. The cannon on the walls all let go. The
balls fell short and over. The mud and snow flew. They
were all like boys at play, hurling epithets as well as shot.
John Henry liked the sport and he was disgusted with
Arnold for losing his temper. Arnold had trafficked in Quebec before the war—making shrewd Connecticut-Yankee
horse trades—and now the English yelled "Horsejockey!"
at him from the walls. Anticlimax with a vengeance!

Arnold retreated twenty miles to wait for Montgomery,
the pockmarked conqueror of Montreal, who arrived
December 1st. Meanwhile, John Henry was wise enough
not to let a heavy-armed Irish colleen trap him down in
her cellar. The army waited for a snowstorm to deliver the
attack. With Montgomery's force, they were eleven hundred strong now.

The white storm came with the new year. At two
o'clock in the morning, Arnold led his men through the
level arrows of the snow. The powder dampened their
coats. Bedlam broke loose. John Henry ran into a ship's
hawser in the dark and had a great fall. Arnold got a can-
nonball in the knee and had to be taken back on men's
shoulders. The Americans could not see whom to shoot in
the dark and snow. They wrenched dry guns from the
British to replace their wet and useless ones. The outer
defenses were taken. Montgomery, leading the attack on
the other side of the town, received in his middle the loading of a cannon set off by a retreating drunken sailor, and
died instantly. Arnold's soldiers found the inner barricades
too high. They were shot down like cattle in the narrow

streets. The high windows belched death. Some Americans escaped along the bay ice. Two hundred men were killed. But even more Britishers companioned them in death next day, to await spring, unfrozen ground, and burial. Dan Morgan was taken alive, and John Henry. The victory over the forest was made a mockery.

The survivors settled down to prison life. John Henry's breeches were gone to tatters, so he joined Dan Morgan in an Indian apron. The prisoners, being Americans, did a deal of whittling. Smallpox mowed the Virginians and only twenty-five of them ever saw the Old Dominion again. A plot to set Quebec afire and escape to Arnold's force was discovered. The men wore heavy irons and chains after that. Spring brought scurvy. John Henry was deathly sick. In May, two war vessels reinforced Quebec and the tatters of Arnold's host were driven away. The prisoners were freed from their irons, got shirts and chewing tobacco. August saw them paroled and embarked. They arrived off New York just a year from the beginning of their campaign and just in time to see the whole town burn to ashes. They were landed in Jersey. Morgan and John Henry leaped out, fell on Jersey, kissed it, and embraced it with their arms. Morgan promised John Henry a good berth in his future company.

But John Henry never filled it. His scurvy came back, his joints were affected, and he went on crutches the rest of his life. He lived, though, to become a famous judge.

Although they did not get Quebec, the lamed John Henry and the lamed Arnold won the right to be called tall sons of Maine, in memory of their Quebec journey. And Jeremiah Getchell.

# 12   Aaron Burr
## Loved a Queen

The fifth tall child of the Kennebec, maybe, was a queen.

History has a way of choosing the wrong people as the leading actors in a play. It chooses the men who have the commissions in their pockets and the epaulets on their shoulders. So it is with the invasion of Quebec of 1775–1776 by way of the Kennebec. To be sure, the man in epaulets this time turned out to be the Judas Iscariot of American history. Still, Arnold is the center-stage man and it may be that he steals the glory from a more significant person, from a New World Amazon of Swan Island who passed like one of the wild white swans up her river to death and to oblivion.

Jacataqua, queen of the Kennebecs, may not be in the official history of Arnold's expedition, but she shines like a star in the oral tradition of the Kennebec. She has a more solid historical foundation, says Charles E. Allen, historian of Pownalborough, than Plymouth Rock. Jonathan Reed, an old Pownalborough man, told Allen the bare bones of the story. "My grandfather," said he, "well remembered Arnold's vessels, and with him was a good-looking young man named Burr, who married a half-breed girl who lived on Swan Island. He took her to Canada and she never came back."

The good-looking young man was Aaron Burr, the second American traitor-to-be of the Kennebec expedition, and the half-breed was the last queen of the once great empire of the Kennebec Indians. So glory fades.

There is another account that does not get into the
history books, either. General Dearborn, who ought to
know something about it since he was a member of
Arnold's expedition, on a visit to his old Gardiner home
around 1827, told the whole story of the lovely Diana of
the Kennebec, who was part French, part Indian, a mighty
huntress of old Pownalborough. He told about Burr's
attachment to her and about her famous English bloodhound. Dearborn had a favorite dog on that trip, but his
dog was eaten when supplies ran short on the bitter march
through the snow. But not Jacataqua's bloodhound. He
arrived whole at Quebec.

The beautiful Kennebec queen faded out, as a queen in
on oral ballad might fade, into many haunting tales along
the Kennebec. But Allen came upon a stirring reconstruc-
tion of this lost chapter of Maine history in the *Maine
Standard* in the year 1867. He thinks, maybe, it was written by a minister of the gospel, Reverend William A. Drew.
Anyway, the story fits Burr with a peculiar appropriateness,
it fits the spirit of Arnold's expedition, and it reads like
gospel truth. It has a further touch of the opéra bouffe
that makes it ring all the more like truth. Our hero-
ancestors in knee breeches and white perukes had red
blood in them. Even in the midst of war and in the heart
of the forest, they could go on a holiday from Puritan
morality and have a good time. The story of Jacataqua
is something of a comic interlude in the Revolution. It
is more. It is an American tragedy, too. The end of
Jacataqua, as of all the women whose lives touched Burr's,
was a tragedy. And behind the bright story is the whole
elegy of the lost splendor of the Indian race. Jacataqua is a
symbol of the betrayal of the natural nobility of the red
men.

Here goes for the story of a queen, as legend has pre-
served it and history has not. Jacataqua belongs in literature. There she can put Pocahontas and all other Indian
princesses in the shade.

One sunny autumn day, a young soldier in buff and
blue was hunting among the starry frostflowers of Swan
Island. He was a long way from home. He was only on
the first rungs of his career. A desperate adventure loomed

before him. But he walked like a young god. Burr's head, even this early, was probably full of the future, when he might stand head and shoulder above all the citizens of the New World.

And then out of the woods burst a woman built like a queen, a Kennebec Diana, with Indian beauty and French on her face, running like a deer, a slim bloodhound baying at her side, a crown of peacock feathers on her head that must have cost a pretty penny in Paris. She was a queen, it turned out, the last of the Kennebec's royal line, the empress of Swan Island. It was enough for Aaron Burr. It was fate. He felt like a future king and here was his queen. The highway of the Kennebec suddenly turned into a swan-road, leading on to glory.

Overhead, the wild swans were slanting down the evening sky when Aaron walked back to his boat with a peacock feather in his hat and the wild touch of the woodland still vibrating on his arms. He had plunged like a swimmer into centuries of graceful and stern living under the sky and stars, into a New World symphony, and his young body was full of the music.

Later, there was a great to-do at Fort Western. There was a queen to be bowed to by bigwigs who wore swords at their sides, slender-stemmed glasses to be drained and snapped so that they might never be drunk from again, and a whole army buzzed with romance.

Judge Howard was having a terrible time with his corn. It eared up beautifully. But something was breaking it down each night and ripping the milky ears apart. It couldn't be woodchucks, it was broken off too high. The devil was to pay and no pitch hot. Aaron Burr waved the judge away. The judge need trouble himself no longer. Burr would put things to rights. He hallooed to Swan Island for his queen. Jacataqua came over. It was swan's feathers today. Her skirts were caught up to her golden knees and she had her long French musket in the curve of her arm. Burr put on his black breeches and his best blue coat. He took an ax for himself. They set out together through the liquid gold of a Maine September day toward the judge's cornfield.

They found the broken stalks. A bear stood up head

and shoulders above them and two cubs nuzzled her side
with wide eyes. Jacataqua threw up her musket and fired.
The bear staggered back among the broken cornstalks. The
cubs fled up a tree. Burr strode in to finish off the monster.
The mother bear took him in her arms and began to tear
the clothes slowly from his body. The black trousers ripped
apart. The cubs leapt from the tree and joined the mother
in her mortal embrace, with claws and teeth like knives.
Then Jacataqua sprang. The long French musket whirled,
there was a dull crack. All the life flowed out of the bear's
eyes. She let go her prey, took two dance steps to the left
and to the right, shook her head once, puzzled, then collapsed like a mountain. Burr shook himself and split one
cub at the skull; Jacataqua laid the other dead with her
musket's butt. She held out her arms, and the exhausted
young soldier wilted away in warm loveliness.

Next day, there were bugles shrilling under the tall
pines and drums going it beside the walls of Western. A
dozen long tables were spread with white under the blue
autumn. The fields were alive with soldiers and rustling
with the wide skirts of fine ladies from Gardinerstown and
Hallowell and Richmond. Little Tory boys crouched in the
thickets and smelt their fathers' potatoes roasting in their
skins in a dozen fires. The three bears of Jacataqua and
Burr were being barbecued in the Indian fashion by Captain Dan Morgan's Virginia riflemen. They were scorching
off the hair and hide, tearing out the entrails, and roasting
them whole. The whole afternoon smelled of bear. The
Indians grunted in anticipation where they sat cross-legged
on the grass. The little Tory boys had water in their
mouths and tears in their eyes. The slabs of reeking bear
meat were carried on birch poles to the table. Twenty baskets of Judge Howard's corn—all that the bears had
spared—were brought on, steaming to heaven. Smoked
Kennebec salmon phalanxed the tables, baskets of wild
cherries, emerald watermelon, and a hundred Maine
mince pies! The Indians could not sit still. Every so often
they sprang up and whooped. The potatoes, smoking in
their own overcoats, were stolen fruit, mostly from Mr.
Greeley's garden, but he was a king's man and it served

him right. There was beef and pork and bread from the army's stores. The soldiers unbuttoned their tight coats.

All the bigwigs were there, William Gardiner from Cobbosseecontee, Major Colburn, Squire Oakman of Gardinerstown, Judge Bowman, Colonel Cushing, Captain Goodwin, maybe of the Yankee-Doodle Goodwins, Edmund Bridge of Pownalborough. And all the bigwigs' ladies. Their hair stood up like baskets of snow. There was one vacant chair, the chair of Parson Bailey of Pownalborough. Probably he was somewhere praying for George III.

Judge Howard sat at the head of the head table. He had a queen on his right, Jacataqua, with her peacock feathers brushing the lower branches of the pines. Burr was on the judge's left. His black breeches were whole again. Jacataqua had mended them. He had on his blue coat, with the swallowtails and gilt buttons on them just where the back of his chair came, his buff-colored best, white stockings, and silver buckles at his knees and shoes. He outshone the October sunlight. Arnold sat at the other end of the table in full regimentals, with some touches of color of his own. Colonel Greene, Captain Enos, the flower of the cavaliers of the South, Captain Morgan, and other officers filled in between. Virginia and Maine, Connecticut and Pennsylvania, sparkled side by side. It was the most famous dinner party ever given on the Kennebec.

The Reverend Samuel Spring, a relative of Burr's and Arnold's chaplain, said grace. He referred to the lovely queen of the Kennebecs along with God. He finished. The lid came off. Knives flashed, and wit burst into flame. Dr. Senter—whose name is on the point of pines opposite the loveliest of Kennebec farms, which happens to be mine— Arnold's head surgeon, appropriately carved. There were toasts and speeches galore. Jacataqua was called on. She gave them: "A Burr, full of chestnuts!" All the guns of Fort Western went off. The echoes rolled up and down the beautiful valley. When the echoes died, all the fifes and drums struck up "Roslin Castle." Amid cheers, Burr rose and lived up to his queen. "I give you," he said, "the Queen of the Kennebecs—may she always have a lapful of chestnuts, fresh from the Burr!"

It was a dinner to remember through ten wars.

When the bateaux were loaded, there was a tall Amazon along, with her English bloodhound. With flashing oars, an army and its queen started on the road to Quebec.

After the river came the forest. Then snow, floods, and disease, then hunger, then starvation, then sleep under the snowy furs, and death, and the wolves howling along the night under the hungry stars. The army dragged itself through the snow, the thousand men dwindled to half that number. The dogs were killed and eaten. Dearborn's pet and others, but the English bloodhound went along alive. The St. Lawrence at last, the River of Death, glittering under the dance of the auroral dead men.

A few days after Arnold's army came out on the Plains of Abraham, there was a strange rendezvous in the forest. Burr was dipping up water in his cocked hat for his queen when a redcoat came up and saluted him and spoke him fair, offering Burr his drinking cup. The Britisher was in a daze over the beauty of Jacataqua. The three became fast friends. They met again and again by the forest brook. They laid plans for Jacataqua's future and for friendship after the end of the war. The Scottish soldier of the king promised to look after Burr's lady, should anything happen. She was great with child. When Burr left with dispatches to General Montgomery at Montreal, the British officer put Jacataqua in a nunnery in Quebec, to lie in. When Burr returned as aide-de-camp to Montgomery, he renewed the secret friendship and saw Jacataqua often during the winter.

Quebec was lost. The Americans retreated. But the Kennebec queen gave birth to Burr's daughter, the Chestnutiana. It was the last touch of comedy in a tale turning tragic as the wind around the eaves in a Maine winter.

The legend thins out. The threads are broken and lost. Silence and mystery close in. Whole years are lost. There are only whispers.

But one whisper tells how a proud queen, befriended by the British officer, came to rejoin Burr on Long Island in a house he had prepared for her, by way of Montreal,

Champlain, and the Hudson. The whisper tells how she was kept there like a dark secret, a wild creature of the forest, tamed and dulled and broken. The bitter years went by. Burr embarked on his double and triple secret ways. Whispers say there were other children by the hidden and lost queen. Whisper claims a prominent New York family descends from the Kennebec queen. There came that black day of disgrace when Burr turned with a smoking pistol, to pass out of the midst of American heroes, to be remembered among the backhanded and the villainous and sinister spirits. And the saddest whisper of all says that when the lost queen heard of Burr's slaying of Hamilton from Burr's lips, she went to Hell Gate in the East River and threw herself in. So ended, whisper says, the queen of the Kennebecs.

The whispers grow thinner and more mysterious about the child. The British officer, they say, went home to Scotland, wounded, in 1783, and took the child as his own with Burr's consent. He educated her and married her off well, other whispers say. Burr visited her, after his disgrace, so it is said. But hard times came, the officer lost his fortune, emigrated to New York. Burr visited him and his daughter there. But the story grows confused and the shadows close over all.

Yet there is a last and deepest whisper of all that tells a terrible story, how a man who had once shone like the sun in the young days of his young country but was tarnished of name and fame now and loaded with infamy, lay paralyzed and helpless, deserted by his last few friends, in his own law office. And one day there came a strange, beautiful, and sad woman, past middle life now, and took Burr home with her to the old Jay Mansion, near Bowling Green. The whisper tells how she took care of Burr in his last two years. And the whisper fades out with the name Chestnutiana.

So queens end, and so dreams of young men who see empires before them, who bathe like swimmers in the clean strength of a forest culture thousands of years old.

# 13 The Naval Battle on the River

Every river worth its salt ought to have at least one sea fight. The Kennebec had one, at its mouth, and it was a ring-tailed beauty. It was fought in the days when strong men fought with cutlasses and could see the color of one another's palates. The days when wooden ships came right up to each other till their cannon touched, and then pounded each other till the ocean was full of dust and splinters. We shall never have such sea fight again.

To be sure, the beginnings of the Kennebec fight were a bit dubious. The whole affair had international complications. Possibly the people of Bath were hoping the British ship would knock the stuffing out of the Yankee one from Portland, that afternoon of the 5th of September, 1813. It seems that the British brig *Boxer* was convoying American ships loaded with British woolens from Halifax to Bath, to keep the Yankee citizens from the winter cold. Woolens were scarce in the new nation. They had to be imported from England; now there was a war and they were contraband. But Bath citizens and the British Navy had a gentlemen's agreement, so that American vessels carrying woolens were not molested. And to make sure the American naval vessels should not pick off the American wool-ships, the British thoughtfully furnished convoys. It had become a regular feature of Maine's seacoast life. The *Boxer* had just brought in some American merchantmen safely and sent them up the Kennebec rejoicing. In order to have all the niceties of decorum observed, the British had fired a few shots over the ships they had so carefully

escorted, as if they were in hot pursuit. but they took care
to shoot at the evergreen headlands a mile or two away.
The Americans had sailed up the river and the British tars
had gone ashore in their boats, probably to do some huck-
leberrying. It was the season for it and there were some
nice big ones at the Kennebecs's mouth.

Those guns they fired were unlucky ones. The sound
of them carried to Portland. There was an American brig
there, the *Enterprise*, just spoiling for a fight. She came
right up to investigate. The *Boxer* saw her coming and fired
her guns to recall her boats, crowded on all her canvas, and
bore down on the *Enterprise*. Captain Blyth was a young
captain, only twenty-nine, and he was ready for a lark any
time. The only trouble was that the *Enterprise*'s captain,
Captain Burrows, was a year younger, and even more in
love with larks. He cleared his decks for action, hung out
the hammocks to keep the splinters down, and set out a
tub of grog amidships for refreshment between shots. The
American sheered away toward Monhegan. The Britisher
pursued, thinking the Yankee's feet were rather cold. That
wasn't the case. Captain Burrows was maneuvering to get
sea room. The wind was light, there was hardly any sea
running. It was going to be a beautiful afternoon's sport.

At three of the ship's clock precisely, Captain Burrows
shortened sail and turned on his pursuer. For twenty minutes the two tall men-of-war closed grandly in. One of the
lime-juicers had gone aloft and was nailing the royal jack to
the mast. It looked like business. They were close enough
at last to see the gold knots on the British captain's wide
hat. There was no mistaking the captain, his hat was wide
as his shoulders, and he was gorgeous as a new butterfly.
Captain Burrows had a new gun he was itching to try out.
It was a long one, mounted in his own cabin, and its nose
poked out the stern window. The Yankee captain wanted
to get the Britisher where he could use it on him.

They were within a half a pistol shot now. Captain
Burrows was gorgeous, too. No one could miss those spot-
less white thighs of his. Each captain waited for the other.
They finally threw up their arms together and both ships
let go at once. Two flowers of yellow flame blossomed at

their sides and spread through the lower rigging of both brigs. They had pistils of white lightning in them. The decks blossomed into shattered wood, the splinters sang like yellow jackets over the sea. At the very start, the British Captain Blyth got an eighteen-pound cannon-ball amidships, fell to his deck half cut in two, and died instantly.

Half-naked men, greased to their eyeballs, ran shot up to the guns, rammed it home, and yanked on the tackling. The guns swung round in the smoke, went forward and poked their noses through the ports, and let fly. They came back too fast to see, swinging a quarter circle, and cried for more. Water was doused on them, and new powder and iron fed down their throats. The ships were so close their splinters mingled. The afternoon was like an unbroken cataract of thunder. Portland heard the cannon, thirty-five miles away. People rushed to the shores of the lower Kennebec to see the fight. The crosses of St. Andrew and St. George leaned in almost touching the flag with the circle of stars above a single thundercloud full of lightning off toward Monhegan.

Captain Burrows had the wind with him. He had seen to that. He ran his brig a bit ahead in the smoke, crossed the lime-juicer's bows, and brought his cabin pet to bear. He let his darling go. There was a sound like a thousand brass kettles and the lime-juicer's foremast buckled and gave a lee lurch toward Sawyer's. Burrows and his gunners yelled for glee and stuffed their gun's belly full again. They swung her about and pulled for dear life to get her long snout out through the window. Captain Burrows put a leg up on the bulwarks to get more of a purchase to pull. He heaved and heaved at the risk of splitting his new breeches stem to stern. And a yowling piece of canister came in through the window, struck Burrows on his straining thigh, and glanced up into him. He went to his cabin floor in the midst of his blood. His men lifted him, to take him below. But Burrows would not go. He was dying. But he swore he would die on the gun deck and see the British strike their colors first. There was no arguing with him. The men left him there among the mad hornets of steel and wood singing around him. They went back to the gun and fed it iron. They poured the hot iron into the Britisher's hull. The foremast was hit twice again. A great net of upper rigging fell into the mass of snarling British seamen. The decks, when the smoke rifted, were cluttered with dead and dying. The *Enterprise* got a ball through her mainmast and one through her foremast. Sailors were crawling on their hands and knees. but the long gun sang like a lark over all the other cannon going. It was music to the dying captain's ears. It raked the British full length. It worked fast, for the captain had not many minutes to live.

At four of the clock there came the hail that made Burrows lift up his sagging head. "They surrender!" the Yankees shouted. The Britisher had got her bellyful of fighting. The officer now in command yelled through his trumpet that he had had enough. He yelled to the Americans to cease firing so that he could unnail his colors and strike them! The Americans roared with the humor of it. But the greasy men stopped serving the guns, wiped the sweat and grime out of their eyes, and felt in their trousers for a chaw of tobacco. "By God! we got the limey!" The smoke lofted slowly and rolled off on the sea.

A tall British officer jumped on a capstan and flourished his heavy meatcutter around his head. "No! no! no!" he shrieked. "We don't surrender, God damn ye!" He went on cussing the Americans up into a peak and frothing at the mouth. But somebody reached up and took him down and carried him away. The Yankees roared again with laughter. A royal tar high up in the tangled rigging tore down the British jack.

One American sailor was dead, three dying, and ten or so more were sprawled about much the worse for wear. The British deck was a shambles.

They brought the dead Blyth's sword to the dying Burrows. He took it in his shaking hands. "Now I am satisfied," He said. "I die contented!" He lingered on for some hours. When the high September stars were out full force he slipped his young cables and went out to overtake Blyth on the great sea where all good sailors go.

They took the prize to Portland on September 7th.

There was a vast turnout, the city crowded the docks. Two
coffins were loaded on two barges hung with mourning.
The sailors in them rowed slowly by minute strokes. All the
other boats in the harbor fell in behind them. Blyth and
then Burrows and then all the rest. They rowed to the
dock. All the bells in Portland tolled. It was the most magnificent funeral ever seen in the city. There was a long procession. Up Fore and Pleasant, onto High, along Main and
Middle, to the meetinghouse. The guns of the Artillery
Company boomed out minute intervals. The procession
began again. It marched to the cemetery on the Eastern
Promenade. The American coffin was followed by American sailors and the British by royal seamen.

A small Portland boy named Henry was there, round-
eyed, and saw it all. He was one day to become America's
great poet.

> I remember the sea-fight far away,
>   How it thundered o'er the tide!
> And the dead captains, as they lay
> In their graves o'erlooking the tranquil bay
>   Where they in battle died.

The two young men were buried side by side, like
good friends forever in death.

> And the sound of that mournful song
> Goes through me with a thrill;
> "A boy's will is the wind's will,
> and the thoughts of youth are long, long thoughts."

# 14 Cap'n Bibber's 'Constitution' Lecture

People still talk about the time Cap'n Cy Bibber gave a lecture on the gun deck of the United States frigate *Constitution*.

*Old Ironsides* was paying a visit to Bath, on the Kennebec, a few summers ago. Everybody went aboard her. Cap'n Bibber did. He took a lot of interest in everything. He squeezed his way through the crowds and pointed out the crowns with GR over them cut into the breeches of the guns. "Limejuicers, every damned one!" he said. Nobody had noticed the crowns before. People got to following him around. He knew where the things were to see. There was a midshipman fresh from Annapolis in the middle of the gun deck. He was giving a lecture to the three or four hundred visitors who had crossed in there. He was telling them all about the old guns and how they were fired.

Cap'n Bibber stood it as long as he could. Somebody had just asked the midshipman what that corkscrew thingamajig over there was. The midshipman shook his head. "Nothing important." He did not know what it was.

"That's the unloader," Cap'n Bibber piped up.

"The unloader?" the middy swung on the Kennebec fisherman. He had been bothered long enough by this man talking on the outskirts of his audience. "Use a bit to unload a gun!—that's a good one, wise guy! A bit! Say, they weren't shooting snowballs, you know!" He laughed his young laughter. The crowd chimed in.

"See here, little one." Cap'n Bibber pushed through the people and stood beside the officer. "Did you think they rolled them cannonballs right into the muzzles like so many dry peanuts. Put your hand out, feller, and see if you're in bed! What do you think would happen when a ship pitched? Them balls would roll right out overboard. They wan't fighting in a washtub, you know, or on no millpond. They was fighting in the sea. Them balls had to be rammed in tight, little one. They wrapped them up in a wad of old cloth—somebody's shirt or something—and they drove them balls in hard. When they didn't use them, they had to have that auger there to draw the charge. And I'm telling you it took a lot of guts."

The midshipman was furious. He got red as a beet. "You," he sneered, "what do you know about sea-fighting in eighteen-twelve?"

Cap'n Bibber waved him back.

"I know plenty. And you don't know nothing. I've stood here and listened to you passing out your spiels long's I could. Now, little one, you stand back and I'll tell these good people where you've made your mistakes. You had your chance. Now you go set down and listen, and I'll tell them right."

The officer looked as if he wanted to hit Cap'n Bibber. But the crowd, sensing that they had an expert in their midst, roared for the middy to let Cap'n Bibber talk.

So Cap'n Bibber talked.

"Here's where Little One here made his first mistake," the fisherman said. "Them tracks are for swinging the guns round so's they could stuff her down the muzzle, all right. But they didn't have to use them blocks and tackle to pull her back. She come back like greased lightning. She come back sudden. When she bellered, she hit her tail at the same time and was sitting turned round all pretty ready for another lot of fish chowder. No. Them tackles was for getting her snout out through the port after she was loaded. Not after she was fired, little one."

For over an hour, Cap'n Bibber stood up there in the middle of an admiring crowd and the sea fights of the War of 1812 came to life while he spoke. He held his listeners spellbound. The midshipman sneaked away and let him tear. It had been his bad luck to start to lecture before the best authority on the gunnery of 1812, and all other years, the whole length of the Kennebec. The captain got pitch-hot when he got well into his speech. He ran up to the guns and yanked and pulled and became an 1812 sailor till the sweat ran down. The crowd cheered and cheered him when he finished. It was a red-letter day in Bath history. They still tell about it.

A short time ago, I met the commander of the *Constitution* at tea. I couldn't help it. I up and told him about how Cap'n Bibber took over the lecture on his ship that day.

"It doesn't surprise me any," said the commander. "If a boy eleven years old couldn't tell most midshipmen I know things they never heard tell of about guns, I'd say he was a dull boy!"

# 15 The River That Flowed Over the World

When the Revolution ended and the Americans stood up as a nation, something tremendous happened to the Kennebec. It started rising, and it kept on rising until its waters covered the Atlantic, poured down around the Horn, out across the Pacific, and met themselves coming around Good Hope. It had circled the globe and neighbors in Bath and Bowdoinham said how-do-you-do to one another in every port of the world. The Kennebec fishing, lumbering farmers suddenly turned sailors, took down the pines back of the barn, and sailed off on them to become citizens of the universe, with their arms in spices of Java to their elbows, in tea of China, and molasses and coffee and sugar of Brazil. For a century, the doorway of the Kennebec stood open and ships came out in thousands and whitened all the oceans with sail, filled the most lonesome waters with songs of sailors and hails to passing ships, and Kennebec men and women and children kept house around the world. Small farmers of Topsham walked, all Yankee spick-and-spanness, by the palaces of Venice and the hovels of Calcutta, through New Orleans and London and Batavia, like the princes they were. A fisherman hung up his shad net and threw a net across the sea and brought back a fortune for his family. The Kennebec became known as one of the chief rivers on Earth. And Kennebec ships were other names for honesty and efficiency and beauty.

The story is almost an incredible one, like most chapters in the swift history of our changing nation, which crowds into a century a thousand years of progress in other lands. From log cabins to the white monoliths of New York almost in the span of one man's life. From narrow little farmhouses on the Kennebec to palaces of high spars moving over the seven seas. It is America and the Kennebec shipbuilding is a part of it.

The beginnings had been humble enough, though from the first Kennebec men had turned to building ships. The *Virginia* of 1607 had numerous progeny. Phips had sailed to a baronetcy on one. But England had stood in the colonists' way. She wanted to make all the colonists' kettles and plows, and she also wanted to bring them over in her own bottoms. But once the apron strings were broken, the Americans burst out all over Britannia's domain. A town with an old English name was the spark that started the blaze of glory. What is now the city of Bath was bought for a song by Robert Gutch, in 1661, from the Indian chief Robin Hood. It had remained one of the many quiet hamlets growing up along the river is spite of the Indians and hard times. But with the end of the Revolution it suddenly found itself a focal point in the growth of a nation reaching out quickly on the seas. It had miles of waterfront, creeks and coves, deep water, though miles from the sea, and water open even in the hardest winters. It had a forest hundreds of miles deep coming right down both sides of the river to its back doorstep. Best of all, it had a peculiar kind of Yankee in it, quick as quicksilver in his mind, full of Yankee love of mechanical gadgets, downright and solid and honest, and yet full of imagination and daring. That was all that was needed.

The people rolled up their sleeves and sailed in. Every man who had a farm with its feet in the Kennebec built himself a set of ways, borrowed his neighbors' adzes and mallets, got the oxen dragging down the long logs, and built himself a second house that could go out on the globe where the money was to be made. David Trufant at Trufant's Creek, Davis, Clarke and Lake, Swanton, Clapp, Jonathan Hyde, who had ancestors behind him in

Connecticut, and William King, who had none at all. By 1800, nearly one hundred of the new kind of traveling house had slid into the Kennebec and started off on their travels. They grew rapidly in size, the *Kingston* was four hundred tons. They grew taller and caught more of the wind in their sails. They took Kennebec lumber and Kennebec fish to the West Indies; the lumber, bought for $8 a thousand, sold for $60. They brought back sugar, molasses, and rum. Many of them paid for themselves in one trip. They began to nose their way across the Atlantic to England and beat the English at their own national game of commerce.

William King was a fair sample of the Yankee builders of Bath. He had his hand in shipbuilding and in almost everything else. He built himself—and he built himself right—on the lines of his own name. Before he finished, he was a king of the New World. First citizen of Bath, first in shipbuilding, first in wealth, first governor of Maine. One day when he was handing his lady into the Boston coach, he discovered a dog there and a Frenchman. "Take this dog out!" he roared. The Frenchmen sprang out and ran for dear life. He said afterward that he had seen lots of kings, the King of France, the King of England, but, said he, "This King of Bath is the biggest king I ever saw!"

William's beginnings were small potatoes. His father died when he was seven. He got his education in a sawmill. At nineteen, he set out from his native Scarborough barefoot and driving all he had in the world before him—a yoke of steers. He was a man about to enter an epic. He set his face toward the rising sun and it landed him in Bath. The ship fever was beginning. William went to work in a Topsham sawmill. In a short time, he owned half a saw, then a whole one, then the whole mill, then the woods behind it. He went down to Bath and opened up a store. Pretty soon he bought up the warehouses, then the wharves, then the ships that landed at them. Then he started building and his ships were soon headed in every direction. One of them, the *Reunion*, paid for itself three times in three successive voyages. William also acquired the bank and a vast kingdom of agriculture. He set out five

hundred fruit trees, and raised potatoes enough to feed the
whole West Indies. He became a major general in the army
and, in 1820, Maine's first governor. He had worked for
years to make Maine independent. He was in everything
and everything he touched turned to gold. He was independent, as Cap'n Bibber would say, as a hog on ice. He
got a law passed that ended town support of the Congregational church. He picked out the best hill and built himself a mansion and furnished it out of the whole world.
Mirrors with the eagles of France, silver dishes, candlesticks
of emperors. And his house became the meeting place of
American culture, with guests entertained as at a palace,
and wines and fine clothes shining. The governor presided
over it all with hair like snow and eyes black as huckleberries and as full of fame as the day he came to Bath driving
his future on the hoof. His word was the law. Yet, though
he lived like a king, he was a democrat to the core and
worked with his hands among his men. Mill worker, store-
keeper, farmer, shipbuilder, soldier, statesmen, artist in fine
living, he was a pattern of Americanism. He is the next tall
son in Maine's long roll of them.

From 1800 on, the Kennebec was crowded with ships
going out from Bath yards. First decade, 38 ships, 43
brigs, 18 schooners, 4 sloops—more than 100 vessels in
all. Second decade, another 100. Third, another. The
1840s saw the number leap to 400, with a tonnage of
88,000, and Bath stood seventh port in the country, after
New York, Boston, Philadelphia, Baltimore, New Bedford,
and Waldoboro. And into Bath came ships of all nations,
English and Spanish and French and Dutch. Bath was a
city of sailors; sailors with strange mustaches and sailors
with rings in their ears. The streets were streets of many
languages. Stories from the corners of the earth and the
smell of strange fruits and tar and new boards. It was the
place for boys to grow up in. Bath became a city and acquired a railroad in 1847, the Portland and Kennebec.

This was the railroad, by the way, that my young great-
uncle avoided riding on to Brunswick and so saved the
quarter dollar that looked as big as a cartwheel to him and
which his father had given him to go hear Jenny Lind sing

in Barnum's circus. And my father, in cap and curls, got
him to help water the elephants and so saved the quarter
again, and they heard Jenny sing like a lark. And my father
persuaded my great-uncle to hoof it back home to
Freeport instead of riding on the Portland and Kennebec,
and so saved the quarter again. And didn't the boy's father
borrow the quarter back from my seven-year-old great-
uncle, and never pay him again! *Sic transit gloria* and New
England thrift.

Bath boomed. There were panics and West Indian pirates, but nothing could stop the city now. The forests
were full of the thunder of falling trees. Yankee ingenuity
was flowering into every kind of mechanical device. Warehouses of ships' supplies sprung up overnight. The city
reeked of hemp and glistened with brass gadgets. Men
good with a jackknife turned out screaming American
eagles and ladies with breasts as big as pumpkins, to go
on ships' prows and cut apart all the winds of the world.
The ships grew larger and larger—500 tons, 800, 1,000.
The *Saratoga* slid into the river, 1,200 tons, in 1849; and
people were there blackening the wharves, from all the
nation, to see this eighth wonder of the world start on her
way.

And Bath wasn't the only place on the river building
ships. Phippsburg, Richmond, Topsham, Bowdoinham,
Hallowell, Augusta, and all the country between. Every
farm that touched the Kennebec had a ship making and
farmers dropping their wheat cradles and taking a turn
with a mallet. A father laid down a keel almost as often as
he begot a son. A new boy and new brig to make him his
living.

Topsham had built a vessel as early as 1768, the *Merry
Meeting*, and all the inhabitants for miles around came to
see it take the water and were fed a huge banquet by the
launching family. Barbecued oxen and mince pies. This
thing became a feature of all Maine launchings, as nowhere
else in the world. A ship launching was a field day, a sermon, a banquet, and fathers came at the heads of their
families in their Sunday-go-to-meeting breeches and their
wives in skirts like apple trees in full bloom. The schooner

*Industry*, built at Topsham in 1772, was the first ship from
the Kennebec to go to the West Indies. When the first
Bath ship, in 1802, was ready to sail, the captain did not
know where his port of New Orleans was. Somebody
thought it was on the Gulf of Mexico. Somebody hunted
up an old Spanish chart. Being a Bath Yankee, the captain
got there, all right. And the first stream of cotton started
north.

Bowdoinham, named for a Huguenot settler, took up
shipbuilding. Elihu Getchell—probably a relation of
Arnold's Jeremiah—built himself a shipyard. Patten's shipyard sprang up and built twelve vessels with names that
give a whole history of American culture, like *Friendship*,
*Industry*, *Menerva*, *Lark*, *Mercury*, *Venus*, *Lucinda*, *Comet*.
The mangrove thickets of the West Indies were full of
Bowdoinham farmers. There was Sampson's yard turning
out the *Olive Branch* and *Sampson*, *Leopard* and *Phenix*, at
Cathance. Purington's yard, Springer's. The Hareward
family yard built 32 vessels. In all, Bowdoinham produced
195 vessels, 55,277 tons of Maine and filled with smart
Maine manhood. This from a town the size of a sleepy
Berkshire village! The fathers had hard work to breed boys
fast enough to keep with the ships' needing young sailors
to live aloft among the albatrosses and stars and see the
world. Bowdoinham, as full of Yankee quirks as a Water-
bury watch, even turned out a "gondola." The thing had
paddles and they were worked by a pair of horses. This am-
phibian creature, hard to classify as either a water vehicle or
a land one, went down the Kennebec beautifully with the
tide. But it never could get back. It stayed down.

Topsham, like Bowdoinham, filled up overnight with
lovely mansions, able to house an army of a family, with
fireplaces in all fourteen rooms and mantels carved better
than Adam could dream, carved by local carpenters who
turned out Greek columns and porticoes better than the
Greeks could do. It was the same story at Bath. The city
grew white in a night and pillars shone along the hills.
Churches shot up, Wren ones, built by the ships; going
and coming below. And the rooms in the houses filled
with carpets woven especially for them in Brussels and

Antwerp, dishes built to splendid Yankee ideas in Bristol and Canton. Furniture came in from palaces at the earth's ends, Sheraton and Hepplewhite and Chippendale, for newer and finer palaces on the Kennebec.

There are more southern mansions in Richmond on the Kennebec than in any southern city under ten thousand population. And Richmond had a population of perhaps fifteen hundred! The reason was, the Richmond people were sea captains and they fell in love with the overhanging portico, with the Greek columns, they saw in Mobile and New Orleans and around there. So they put a Parthenon front on all their houses, even the little ones.

Hallowell and high Gardiner built their ships with the rest of them. Captains had thirty miles of farms to sail through before they got to sea. One Hallowell shipyard built two whole ships, forty-five men working at each, and "without use of ardent spirits!" Maybe a record. The Kempton and Small yard was famous. The *Mary Jane* of Hallowell defied the Embargo Act of 1807, ran under the booming cannon at the Kennebec's mouth, and made a fortune in the West Indies. Captain Gershon Cox made a record. Son of a sea captain, he begot five more famous ones. Another Hallowell master, Shurbael West, saw the sea serpent off Cape Ann. And Captain Llewellyn Cooper, after sailing often round the Horn and captaining a swift London-Calcutta packet, changed with the times to steam and became the best steamship captain on the Atlantic.

The first steamer from Hallowell to Boston started in 1838. A rival soon appeared. Then Cornelius Vanderbilt put a steamer on the route named for him. In the forties, a fourth appeared. It was cutthroat competition. Tickets to Boston were reduced to ten cents and once passengers were paid twenty five cents to go to the Hub!

The shipbuilding was like a fever. Towns far inland caught it. A ship was built at Lisbon, dragged around the Androscoggin Falls by oxen and launched at Brunswick Landing. Brunswick had half a dozen yards going. The climax came when a man built him a vessel in Mair Brook, the trout stream Hawthorne fished in the early twenties! Every man would have his ship!

The peak of the era of wooden ships was the decade
before the Civil War. And Bath, in the fabulous fifties, rose
to be the fifth port of the United States; only New York,
Boston, Philadelphia, and Baltimore ranking it. In 1857,
183,000 tons of shipping were owned in the city on the
Kennebec. One-half of all the American wooden ships were
Maine built and Bath was the capital of this industry:
33,000 tons of ships went down the ways each year. The
ships grew from 1,000 tons to 1,500. America was carrying most of the world's goods and the American merchant
marine stood first in the world, head and shoulders above
the British. It was the Homeric Age of sail.

There were several reasons why America took the lead
with her sailing ships. One reason was cotton in the South
needing manufacturing in England. Another was the apparently unlimited lumber in the forests of Maine and beyond.
Still another was the opening of California and the Pacific
coast to the world. All goods had to be carried around the
Horn, and America was there to carry them. And the
opening of the Pacific coast meant new lumber, and that
lumber was the key that opened China and all the orient to
American sailors. They carried it across the Pacific to sell
and brought back cargoes of tea and silk and spice and rice
and hemp. Fortunes at both ends of the wide ocean.

There were good reasons why Kennebec ships led the
world. One was, they were better ships. They were built
solid, they carried the biggest cargoes, being almost square
in their holds amidships, their masts were very tall, and the
seamen could pile on the canvas to a fare-you-well. And
they did. They went past the best from Bristol and Liver-
pool and were gone over the horizon almost before the
British could call them crazy Yankees. They could be built
more economically than any ships going. They were hon-
estly made, and yet full of gadgets for handling canvas and
making sailing easy. They were as solid as Maine manhood.
And they were beautiful. A bow high and fine and a sheer
like a seagull's wing. The clippers of Newburyport and
Salem could beat them, but those boats carried smaller cargoes, they were for looks more than business, and they had
faded like ghosts when the sturdy Bath ships were still
swinging along on all the seas.

But there were better reasons still. The Maine seamen were the world's best. They were native-born Americans, men with at least a common school education, and ambitious to get on. They were the best paid of all sailors. Yet they followed the sea for the love of it. They were mechanically minded. They were lords of creation, living a hundred feet over the sea on the cobwebs of the rigging, among the American stars and close to the sun. They had the eagle in them and the great American pride.

Their masters were cut from the same cloth. They were not hired men. They were owners or part owners of the ships they sailed. They were business agents in foreign ports. They were shrewd buyers and sellers. they were democrats, and their men were their relatives and their friends. These Maine Yankee shipmasters were unique in still another way. No matter how high they rose or how rich they grew, they never lost their feeling for the land and home. Captains noted in their logs in the Indian Ocean that it was haying time now, back home on the farm, and wondered if the old mare would be able to stand the gaff of getting in the six tons of hay. Or they wondered, in the middle of blistering weather off Brazil, if there were snow enough for good sleighing this January day and what neighbors were eating popcorn balls to the tune of the frosty sleigh bells. These men never got over being farmers and shopkeepers and fishermen. Never stopped being plain Maine folks.

Their Maine ships were unique things. They were not aggregations of the work of specialists. They were built by families. From keel to topmost spar, they were another such thing as a farmhouse. They were members of a family, like a son or a daughter. Sons and daughters often had a share built into them, as they had their own rooms built into the family house when it was going up. Every bit of work that went into them was a labor of love. Many of them were built at home and the children played among the shavings inside the ribs of them just as they played in woodshed or barn.

They were seasonal symphonies, too, these ships. The keel was laid when the grass showed its first green around it. Their planking was finished when the goldenrod

blossomed. And they usually went into the river to meet
the rising of the harvest moon. A launching meant the end
of two seasons of hard work and the friends and neighbors
who ate the sliced turkey there and drank the raspberry
shrub where taking part in a real Thanksgiving feast. There
might be music. There were always prayers and speeches,
and sometimes a whole sermon. There was always cider.
The rigging was up by the time the snow flew and the
other house of the family was ready to go rolling about the
shoulders of the globe; earning the bread and butter, and
the silks and china, too, for the house rooted to the land.
One a year. The years meant so many ships in a man's life.

In many an old Kennebec attic, you will come upon
dusty logbooks. Behind the bold scrawls in unfading ink,
behind the formulas, "Comes in fresh southeast winds,"
latitudes and longitudes set down so scrupulously day after
day, there once was amazing life. Life lived on a scale as
wide as the world. Those small marks mean hard work—
desperate cold work by men going on icy narrow paths
above death a hundred feet below, swaying on an arc
across a quarter of the sky. They mean seas coming aboard
off the Horn and hens and cows swept from the decks.
They mean men going overboard in a desolate waste of
waters and ship tacking back and forth for hours in vain
search. They mean earthquakes in faraway ports and ships
foundering at the foot of strange mountains. They stand
for incredible painted trees and men and cities of Java and
Sumatra. They stand for loneliness and peril, for a year's
work abandoned in a ship with masts shattered and hurricane sails in ribbons. For cities like dreams and albatrosses
floating mournfully under the moon. I read in one such
log the last entry the captain made before he took to the
boats; while the pumps were losing the fight against the
water in the hold, the captain was writing a little essay in
praise of farming and life with one horse, a few apple trees,
and a dozen or so rows of potatoes to tend and hoe.

But the log entries stand for prosperity, too. So many
thousand dollars in the bank for a finer house back home.
For children born at sea. Happy days with a wife darning
the captain's socks and ironing new baby clothes. For these

Yankee captains kept house at sea, around the world. Their wives went along with them oftentimes and made a rolling cabin a home. Many Maine babies were born on the other side of the globe. Maine men went on their honeymoons around the world, in the 1850s. A wife did her family shopping in Venice and Plymouth and Hong Kong. Her home was the wide world.

Bath must have been a fine place to live in, a century ago. The streets smelled of far countries. The shop windows were pages of a geography book. And all day long there was music through the air, the sound of a thousand wooden mallets driving home the treenails in the planking of a dozen hulls. The rhythm of those blows must have got inside the Bath people, and they must have walked like a new kind of men, moving through a world symphony. At the end of every street there were white sails and ships were going by like high summer clouds.

But the days of the square-riggers were numbered. The next decade brought the Civil War and the beginning of the end of the American merchant marine, thanks to Confederate raiders with which an envious England supplied the South. By 1870, Britannia ruled the waves again. There were other ministers of doom. One was that new kind of highway that had come innocently into Bath in 1847. It lengthened out over the land, over the Rockies, and it sucked the life of ships away on the far Pacific at last. It cut across rivers and went down the coasts. And the ships grew scarcer and lonelier on the ocean. And still another minister of doom came bucking up the Kennebec without any sails and reeking with smoke from a smokestack. There were more ships built in Bath in the sixties than the fifties, but the tonnage dropped from 181,000 to 118,000. The vessels were smaller, and they had a different kind of sail. Schooners were replacing ships. They were handier for getting along the coasts. For the ocean of Bath men was shrinking to coastal gulfs and bays. The British were taking back the wide sea.

Bath was hard place to kill, though. The city went bravely on, changing to schooners. New names replaced the old among the yards—Deering and Percy and Morse

and Hude. There was another bit of handwriting on the
wall, the shrinking of the Maine forests. But Bath fetched
her timber from Vermont and Canada and the South, and
went on. Times changed, she shifted her cloth and her scis-
sors with the times. She branched out into a new role and
built two ships for the United States Navy, the *Katahdin* in
'62 and the *Ioseo* in '64, wood still. And she met the challenge of steamers by starting to build them herself, the
*Montana*, '65, the *Idaho*, '66.

In the decade of 1870–1880, Bath broke even the tonnage record of the fifties. But the vessels were smaller. And
Bath was building ships for other seaports, not herself.
Some seagoing vessels were still owned in Bath, but the
number was steadily dwindling. The square-riggers made a
last stand to survive and the few built grew larger, one of
2,000 tons took the ways. Schooners were growing, too,
to tonnage around 1,000. And in the decade 1880–1890,
Bath was a hive of building as never before. She reached
the tonnage peak of her history: 50,000 more than in the
fifties. Morse built ice schooners for the Kennebec ice industry. Seagoing tugs were turned out.

And in 1889, General Hyde, who had made a proud
name for himself in the Civil War, founded the Bath Iron
Works. The last jump was reached, to steel. The first steel
craft were gunboats for the United States Navy. The last
square-riggers grew to more than 3,000 tons. Schooners
grew, too, to 1,600. But they also were doomed. They
were sinking to the ignominy of carrying coal along the
coast. And most of Bath's commerce had been lost to
other ports. Only ice remained. The tugs of the Knickerbocker Towage Company were dragging lines of ice
schooners up and down the river. All the other Kennebec
towns fell silent. The eighties heard the last hammer blows
struck in the shipyards above.

But Bath fought to the last ditch to remain a shipbuilding town. In 1889, Arthur Sewall enticed President
Harrison to Bath to show him the shipyard facilities. The
United States Navy came, too. A vast clambake for the officers was the thing that probably clinched it. From that
time on, Bath was a leading builder for the Navy.

But in the nineties, the wooden ships went out in a last blaze of glory. Sewall's *Roanoke*, 3,539 tons, the largest square-rigger ever built, the schooner *Eleanor A. Percy*, more than 3,400. Nearly 200,000 tons in all, but many of the vessels were steam. The craft were built for other ports, too, and were standardized and impersonal things. The Bath Iron Works went on with warships; steel now. Sewall and Hyde had visions of Bath as a second Clydebank. They kept Bath in the forefront, though the materials came from afar, by sheer Yankee excellence in building traditions. Grandsons of the earlier builders worked still in their yards. And the naval building carried Bath through. From 1901 to 1915, Bath built one monitor, two cruisers, three torpedo boats, eleven destroyers, and one first-line battleship. Don't I recall that bitter day when the battleship *Georgia* went down the ways! For I got there too late to see it go. That has always been the way with me and ships at Bath. I saw it only on the Kennebec, aflutter with pennants, half the world away already. It was a horse's fault. Dick ran away with the buggy while my father and I were getting a drink from the Witch's Spring on the Bull-Rock turnpike, and it took us an hour before we located him in somebody's cornfield with the buggy the worse for going through a narrow gate. It is one of the scars I wear on my mind.

The bottom of Bath building was the first years of the twentieth century. One last great schooner, bigger even than the record ship, was launched in 1909, the *Wyoming*, 3,730 tons and six masts. But it was a last gesture of bravery in a world without wooden ships.

In the war, though, Bath came back to fame. The new Texas Yard was a vast beehive in full bloom. Every farmer's son for miles around earned money for his college education tossing bolts and shoveling up grease from the ways as ship after ship went off to replace freighters sunk by German submarines. A whole new Bath rose in Aladdin houses. The population doubled. But the end of the war saw the new city collapse. The tide is still near the low ebb, though two destroyers were built in 1936 and the keel poured for 1937's America Cup Defender.

Bath is an eloquent empty cradle of a merchant marine that once covered the oceans with white and gilt and smart manhood. The city is like her river. Her greatness is a past greatness. But the seeds of Yankee ingenuity still lie there, waiting, as the river lies waiting, for a new spring in American history.

# 16 King Log

The history of Maine is the history of three kinds of trees. And the Kennebec was the road down which they traveled to become the houses, the ships, the books, and the very lifeblood of men.

The pine at first was king.

Whoever leaves Brunswick by the Bath Road passes, even on the brightest July day, into a lovely twilight in the midst of noon. It is like going into the dusk of the gods, with the sunbeams slanting magically through the high tops of the white pines. Pillars of trunks without a branch rise for seventy feet, and the floor of the forest is made of a thousand years of needles. White-pine forests once stretched across the whole state. This is one grove only, which Bowdoin College has saved. When I was a boy in Brunswick, the pines nearly circled the town and any day when the wind blew, living in Brunswick was like living in an organ. Longfellow walked among these trees that were here before Shakespeare had walked down to London to make his living by writing plays. Many of the Bowdoin pines are older than the white men in America. Elijah Kellogg, another son of the college of pines, preacher, fisherman, and farmer of Harpswell, and a belated saint straight out of Bede's *Ecclesiastical History*, wove them into his boys' books and he has as his monument one of them inscribed with his name. No man could choose a finer thing to be remembered by. Those pines cast a permanent and lovely shadow on the mind of Nathaniel Hawthorne.

The belt of great trees across the lower half of Maine furnished the white and square farmhouses that sprinkle the small Maine villages and towns with squares of rock candy. The tale of their hundreds of years is written in the grains of paneling over fireplaces and in doors inside those houses. Those trees built the houses of the four-footed friends to man, the vast barns, with their ax-hewn beams and two-foot boards without a knot for thirty feet. Even the pasture fences are parts of those pines.

These memorials are left to the vanished forests of Maine. But other parts of that forest are rotting away under every one of the seven seas. For the white pines of Maine furnished the sinews for the hulls of most of the sailing ships of New England, when New England was the cradle of American industry and culture.

Those pines were floated down the Kennebec to be branded with the arrow that meant that they were to be the masts of the Royal British Navy. They held up a mountain of white sails on the American frigates of 1777 and 1812. They went to Java and Sumatra and China, round the Horn, and back by Good Hope. They were near the sea and the Kennebec ran full of them in the springs of all the years to the day when steam came in, and the new iron skin for sea craft. The river furnished the power to bring them down to the shipyards and to lay them open into wide, light boards. The song of the long drivers mingled with the song of the saw, and young Maine ships went away from Bowdoinham and Bath on the high-run tide of every year to carry Maine brawn and energy and love of things shipshape and shining to the four corners of the globe. King Pine flourished when the Kennebec was still a river as clear as crystal and the salmon and the great sea bass followed the keels of ships up to the falls at Augusta. It was a clean tree and the business of turning it into ships was a clean business. These trees stood next to the very yard where they were being turned into ships, they were like tall friends of all the coast men, and they were really the begetters of the many tall young men who went to sea and stood up tall to the world. Their goodness was in the large and lively families they brought into being.

They are gone now, save in a few small groups that men have spared. Landmarks at the Y where three roads meet. But they are eloquent reminders of the day of tall ships and spacious houses in the time of Maine's glory.

The second king was King Spruce.

He was a tougher customer. He came from farther north. He was harder to get down and to kill out. He isn't completely wiped out even today. The giants of his race are gone. But their smaller cousins held on like grim death to the swampy bottom lands at the foot of the mountains of interior Maine. Spruce was a stayer, anyway. The coast kind has sucked its life out of nothing but its own ancestors' bones and bare granite on a thousand and one islands around Kennebec's mouth and the rest of the coast and has kept its legions unbroken ever since the white man came.

Spruce was never so tall as white pine and was used for less lofty things than ships and Maine barns. Its coarser grain was built into less pretentious forms, where beauty of line was not needed. It spread out into warehouses and factories across the United States. Kennebec spruce meant good, stout, and honest roofing over a man's head as he walked back and forth at a loom. It meant sound ties under a train. Utilitarian Monday and Tuesday things. Yeomanly wood for yeomanly purposes.

Spruce came into the cycle of harvest after the best of the princes of pine were gone. It had farther to travel by water, from Moosehead all the way down to the middle towns. It came from the lonely places where bear and deer were the only householders and the trout shone with watery rainbows under their fins in clear, running brooks. It hailed from the moose country, where the giants of Maine wildlife marched through the swamp grass with a tree on their heads that was blood brother to its own spiky boughs. The only men it saw, before the day of its doom, when it went down like thunder into the snow, were the gum gatherers. These stalwarts came, mustached in the Victorian mode and armed with long poles wet with blades. They cut off the lavender knobs of its blood, flecked with tiny blazing suns of new pitch, and collected the fragments of gum in their knapsacks, to strengthen the jaws of all Americans, to whiten American teeth, and put

on American tongues the tang of the very essence of sharp
and fragrant Maine. The new tips of spruce boughs were
used for making beer, too; good lusty brew for the spring
of the year. It was bottled in stone crocks and it tasted
wild. My father brought his sons up on it.

The era of spruce was the era of the beginning of the
pollution of the Kennebec. The sawdust from its boards
was dumped into the river along with the dyes and chemi-
cals of the paper mills beginning to poison the river in the
seventies and eighties of the nineteenth century. The
spruce was less clean than the pine. It marked men's hands
with stains that defied even the homemade soft soap. But it
also made its tough men, giving work and wage to thousands of people, until it, too, began to peter out.

The third king of the Kennebec was King Pulp.

Pulp means every kind of tree from spruce and fir to
popple. It is the only harvest of wood left. Shortsightedness and the lumber merchants' impatience have brought
down the chief Maine industry of the latter part of the
nineteenth century to such small pickings. The small logs
were cut up and peeled, rolled into the streams, and
floated to the rivers when the thaws came. And the small
streams of both the Kennebec and the Androscoggin
drained the last life of Maine's once magnificent forests
away. Wood to be the shoddy annals of shoddy living. Even
a popple must blush. In the freshet season, the small pulp
logs came down the Androscoggin and Kennebec like pro-
jectiles. They could shoot through the windows of a
flooded mill and out of the widows at the other side. They
vented their wrath on the mills where they were destined
to go, the mills that vomited purple dyes and rank chemi-
cals into the river and dealt death to the last descendants of
the noble salmon and bass and shad that used to fill the
river with islands of silver. The floods often took the pulp
sticks fanwise out into the Atlantic. And the fishermen
gathered them for firewood on the far islands. These logs
were so small that they traveled without man's help to the
places of their destruction.

But it was not so in the days of the Maine fathers and
grandfathers and great-grandfathers. Then the forest and

the river that was the high road out of it were pages out of Homer.

The epic began with women packing up bacon and woolen underwear in the time of the first spitting of the snow in hundreds of small farmhouses across the state. For, as always, Maine men were Jacks-of-all-trades. Farmers in the one month between frosts, which is called summer, hunters in the fall, lumbermen in the winter, ice loaders in the spring. The men of hundreds of families went walking off into the November dawn with felts and rubbers on their feet and a great smoke of breathing around them. Yellow and brown mustaches and many more black ones, for a great many of the men were ones who had stemmed from "P.Q."—the Province of Quebec—and who had followed the Maine rivers down from the forests of the St. Lawrence, who spoke Canuck, and who handled their slim symphonies of curving wood and steel, their axes, as if they were attractive and tender young women.

The men might have to tramp a hundred miles to get to their trees, but they got there. They filled the silence between the mountains with the sound of their axes and the sound of falling trees. They went at it with cant dogs and mustaches straining like the antennae on fierce insects. They flowered the virgin snow with sunflowers of tobacco juice. They shouted and cussed and sang. They scared the rabbits out of trefoil tracks into parallel ones. They got down a lot of logs from sun to stars. And they filled their brush-banked log cabins with the heat of their bodies and tobacco smoke you could cut with a knife. They told stories and downed dough-devils that would sink an iron ship. It was in these little cramped cabins beside lonesome miles of ice on lost lakes that Paul Bunyan cut his teeth. Paul Bunyan, whose mother rocked him in a hollow Maine pine so hard that she set the tides running fifty feet high in the Bay of Fundy. You can go and see them if you don't believe it. Paul, by the way, is no relation of John Bunyan.

Paul didn't stay in Maine. The trees got too few and far between for him. He lit out on the logging trail to the Great Lakes and followed the good timber west till he brought up on Puget Sound, cutting Douglas fir, which

was never a tree to mention in the same breath with a State
of Maine white pine. That's the way with Maine. She never
could keep a lot of her smartest young ones home. They
went out and founded most of the middle and western
states. There is another good Kennebec crop that once was
bigger than now—men. White pine, spruce, salmon, ice,
and men—the bumper harvests are gone.

When the big stumps began to sweat sweet blood and
the waxen mayflowers gave way to anemones, then the
Kennebec stepped into the story. The ax swingers were
home by then and their money was pretty well gone up the
flue, between wives and children and housekeepers. The
woodchucks were home and the water rats took up the
song. They were leaner and had still wider mustaches, and
their brains ran down into their feet. On a hundred ponds
and streams, the rotten ice let go and long logs came pol-
ing their snouts through the woods in a hurry. The water
rats nursed them out into the white water, where the going
was even faster. The freshets caught the logs up and they
reared on their ends, sleek and wicked, looking for trouble.
They jammed into the backwaters and chewed each other
up into yellow splinters. The men had to run out along
their backs and prod them apart and set them going again.
Their feet were light as cats' as they ran the bobbing logs.
Their feet thought for themselves and danced over the
gaps where the black water showed. The wide-mustached
men rode the wild wooden horses with their feet dangling
in water only a few jumps from freezing. They headed the
logs out of jams. Sometimes they would have to run for
dear life under a wall of hell's babies lifting themselves suddenly twenty feet in the air and bent on snapping the
men's backbones. Now and then a foot slipped and a good
logger went home to a clean river bed of sand and green
music over him for the rest of his time. And maybe a
baker's dozen of bright-eyed Canadian boys had to step all
at once into their father's shoes. And the logs went roaring
down the Kennebec, going over the falls and filling the valley with thunder and white flowers.

Down at the gap at Hallowell, at the log booms, the
down-river men caught the wild horses and sorted them

out. Each log had a brand cut into its bark near the larger
end. The men claimed their own by arrows and crosses and
triangles. They rounded them up, spiked them, and lashed
them together in rafts made up like bunches of firecrackers.
Big end and little end and big, and so on, fastened along
their ends until they made a long boat. The men rowed
them down river, steering them on their way by their
sculls, till they came to the mills.

Then the late spring was a scream of silver saws under
the side roofs around Gardiner. Logs came in on the rol-
lers as gray trees and went out as long leaves of gold and
alabaster. They were piled in the sun with chocks between
to allow them to breathe as they grew old together. Lumber was a spring industry, like the ice. Farmers put off the
plowing to make the money for their seed corn and potatoes, lifting and swinging the new boards ten hours a day,
till their bodies were a fine rhythm and their faces were
brown as the bark the silver teeth tore off the sides of the
boards. The potatoes and beans had to wait till Decoration
Day and after.

I once had an uncle who lived by lumber. He was a
good uncle to have around. He always smelled like newly
sawn boards. He had the strong, clean smell of the pith of
a pine tree. No matter how long he stayed in the house, he
kept that smell of the outdoors on him. He knew how to
handle wood. He cut bits of white pine up into the most
fragile toys of my boyhood. He could make boats that
went one into the other until the last was half the size of a
walnut shell but had just as lovely curves as the first. When
he went, it was like the loss of a forest.

The yellow leavings of the logs poured into the river
year by year, covering over the rich dark feeding grounds
of salmon and trout, killing the fry, carpeting the river with
a carpet of death. The March floods scoured the sawdust
out in places, but there was always more sawdust to come.
And down at Woolwich and Bowdoinham the farmer-
fishermen left their shad nets hanging in the open chambers along with the nets of the spiders, left their boats on
the banks under the birches, and became only farmers.
They pulled in their belts another notch over their flat

Yankee bellies. And next year there were fewer new sons in the cradles and fewer young men walking back from church through the June daisies with their brides on their arms.

The paper mills of Augusta and Gardiner did for the water above the carpet of sawdust and bark. They ate up Maine's wealth in young trees and spewed out their venom and acids, until the hosts of fish hawks over blue Merrymeeting dwindled into squadrons of three and five. There were fewer words of high beauty written on the summer blue, the wings that think independently and move for the sheer joy of moving disappeared from the sky. In the gnarled Norways by Abagadassett River, the thin blue eaglets cried for food. Each year they were fewer. And now the bird that carries a flake of the sun between his wide wings high up against the sun itself, the bald eagle, is a vision of solitary loveliness seen only once or twice a year.

The first paper mills of the Kennebec were cleaner houses of industry. They used rags for papermaking. Whole colonies of English people, at about the time of Waterloo, were imported to work in them by the rapids of the Cobbosseecontee. A part of old England walked along Maine's roads with cheeks like rose hips. It was the old story of many races meeting and mingling to produce the Kennebec people. Catholic French and Protestant English, Scotch and Scotch-Irish, Moravian Germans, Irish, Huguenot French, French-Canadians, and Poles, and Finns and Swedes. Old bloods of Europe, which could no more mingle in the Old World than oil and water, mingled here and made Maine American. The newercome bloods keep more to themselves. But the day of their uniting with the stream will come, as it did in the old days. Sailing ships brought the mills rags in bales from the ends of the earth. Spotted fever came in some of them. And foreign death stalked by the Kennebec.

The rag paper gave place to paper made from Maine's trees. What the lumbermen had left, the papermen stripped from the hills. Great paper mills sprang up at Winslow and Madison. Today, the ospreys and eagles are a rare and haunting sight on Merrymeeting, but people all over the States are able to keep abreast of the nation's scandals and crime, thanks to Kennebec pulp.

King Log is dethroned and his long saga, with the wind running through it and the deep snows of Maine shining through, is gone the way of anemones in the heat of the year. The Kennebec rolls on; but through hills where the great green captains of the forest are gone from the sky.

# 17  Kennebec Crystals

The shopkeepers of Hallowell and Gardiner and
Augusta had watched the January weather like hawks.
They thumbed their ledgers and shook their graying temples at the lengthening columns of debit. The doctors had
their eye on the sky as they felt of their lank wallets.
Twenty miles deep, each side of the river, farmers in small
story-and-a-half farmhouses eyed their grocery-store thermometers at the side door and bit more sparingly into
their B.L. plugs. They chewed longer on their cuds, too.
In the kitchen, the wife was scraping the lower staves of
the flour barrel. The big bugs in the wide white mansions
along the river looked out of their east or west windows at
crack of day to see the state of the water. Teachers in
school grew short with their pupils who confused
Washington's crossing of the Delaware with Clark's fording
the fields around Vincennes. The mild weather continued.
The river rolled on, blue in its ripples. Shopkeepers got
short with their wives.

Then a sharp blue wind came up out of the northwest,
the mercury in the thermometers tumbled. The pines
roared on into the dark, the stars snapped in the sky like
sapphires. Good weather for future soldiers, Napoleon
once remarked. Napoleon be hanged! So thought the
farmers along the Kennebec, who were up in history as
much as they were down in their pork barrels. There were
enough small pairs of pants running around their farms
already. What they needed was nights to breed the life-
giving ice that would keep the small thighs in the trousers
going. Good freezing nights for starting the crop of the
water.

The cold spell was a real one. Farmers had to beat their arms each side of their buffalo coats. Next sundown the wind fell. It got still as a pocket. You could hear the stars sputter over the valley. The shopkeepers sat sipping their evening's lime juice and gloated over their newspapers. "The Hudson Valley: continued mild weather, southerly winds, higher temperatures and showers for next week." It was a different story up here in Maine. The kitchen windowpanes had white ferns at their corners. A knife handle would have to be used on the water bucket in the morning. Down Hudson, up Kennebec! In the morning, there would be no more waves running on the river. The water looked like a long, dark looking glass dropped between the hills. In a hundred sheds the grindstones were humming.

The next day the January thaw came. Teachers went all to pieces as early as Wednesday in the week. Doctors used the whip on their horses as they clattered over the steaming ruts. Shopkeepers did not throw in the extra pilot bread but tied up the bags and bit off the twine. The big bugs behind the Ionian porticoes put aside the *Annals* of Tacitus and took down the *Magnalia Christi Americana* of Cotton Mather and Jonathan Edward's *Sinners in the Hands of an Angry God*. Small boys lost their tempers and kicked the jackstraws their bachelor uncles had whittled out in the shape of oars and ellspears all over the floor. Farmers sat down to Indian pudding without any salt hake to season it off.

Young Timothy Toothaker decided not to ask Susannah Orr a certain question until mayflower time or later. And he stopped spooling new rungs for her future bed.

The thaw lasted eight days. Somebody saw a robin. He didn't get any vote of thanks from his neighbors. A body could see his dead grandmother in such fog as there was. The graybeards by the barrel stove in Ephraim Doughty's grocery store at Bowdoin Center shivered in their shoes. Ephraim had said earlier in the evening, as he looked out at the weather glumly, "Open winter, fat graveyards." Active Frost cheated at checkers and got caught. Wash Alexander drank up all his wife's Peruna.

The only consolation in Kennebec County was the newspaper. It said it was raining all up and down the Hudson, from Saratoga to Staten Island.

February came in murky. But the trotting horses on the Kennebec barns swung round at last and headed north: the thermometer went below zero and stayed there. Everybody began to breathe again and the grindstones started singing.

The Kennebec was gray glass again, next dawn and next and next. It grew blacker as the days went by. In the third night the drums began a single stroke, now and then, low bass and far away, rolling and reverberating along the hills. Next morning there were white cracks on the dark drumhead to show where the drumsticks had struck. All at once, at four o'clock, the whole stretch of the river below the Augusta falls blossomed out with children in bright scarves, just out of school. A thousand young farmers and townsmen ground bark, cut figure eights, and yelled themselves hoarse at Ring-Leavo. Fat boys of six on their first skates stared wide-eyed at the green water weeds hanging still and going down into fearful darkness under their toes. At night, bonfires ran down the river from bend to bend. Flame answered flame from Skowhegan to Swan Island. Everybody but those in slippers and those in cradles was out on the ice. And next afternoon, the horses had taken to the new ice highway that connected all the Kennebec towns. Men flew along behind them, mountains of robes in narrow sleighs. Their big mustaches smoked and their breath clung to them like mufflers straining out behind. Women swept past, little crepe bonnets cocked over the left eye and eyes like jets and blue diamonds. The ice was marked off into lanes, the racing sleighs came out. Horses came up the river, neck and neck, the flowers of their breaths festooned each side of them like garlands hung from high head to high head. Whips cracked and shouts sent out long echoes each way. The chipped ice shone like splinters flying from a rainbow. Young men had young arms around waists of only eighteen inches and young people started off on the road to matrimony on the thinnest of bright steel shoes.

But back up on the farms, the men were grinding their picks. Women were laying out armfuls of gray socks with white heels and toes, piling up the flannel shirts, packing up bacon and ham and sausage meat and loaves. Boys were oiling harnesses and polishing the glass sidelights of

headstalls. Chains were clinking and sleds were being piled
with blankets and bedding and victuals and extra whiffle-
trees, cant dogs, picks, and feed for the horses.

Down along the river, the doors stood open in the big
icehouses with sides lined with sawdust, that for months
had been shut in silence except for the sharp, thin music of
wasps. Men were clearing out old roughage and rubbing
the sections of track free of rust. Machinery was being
oiled. Gouges and scrapers were being looked over and
assembled by the river's side.

The preachers and everybody else in Gardiner and
Richmond, Hallowell and Dresden went to bed that night
praying for the snow to hold up and the red blood in the
glass to stay down in the ball where it belonged. The river
of Henry Hudson was still liquid as it went under the
Catskills and down by the walls of the Palisades. God was
in his heaven!

In the clear dawn next day, along a hundred roads that
led down the Kennebec, farmers were trudging, mustaches
hanging down to the woolen mufflers like the tusks on the
walrus. Brown mustaches, golden ones, black ones, gray
ones, and white. But every one in front of a man. And behind them streamed their wealth, on its own feet. Tall,
sinewy sons, out of school for good and on the doorstep of
manhood and marriage, horses with hides like scrubbed
horse chestnuts, big of hoof and billowy of muscle, fat-
tened on corn, sharp shod, with long calks of steel that bit
into the frozen ground. Here you could reckon up a man's
prosperity in solid, tangible things, as in the days of Jacob
and Laban. Goods with the breath of life in them. Like
Job's. The richest man was one who had nine or ten strong
men to follow the swing of his creasing trousers in ringing,
ironed shoes. Or three or four spans of horses with the
morning star in their foreheads and the music of steel
under their feet. So the wealth of the Kennebec came
down to the harvest of Maine's best winter crop in the
1880s.

Tramps, even, were coming. And all the black sheep of
a hundred faraway pastures, beyond Maine, were swinging
off the sides of freight cars in the chill gray of the morning.
Drifters from far beyond New England.

The men crowded into the river lodging houses of Hallowell and Gardiner, Pittston and Dresden. They unloaded and stowed their dunnage in their temporary homes for the next few weeks. They armed themselves with picks and gougers and saws. Each man had his favorite tool tucked under his quilted arm. They descended on the cold harvest floor with horses and sons in a great host.

Then the field of the harvest was marked off for the game of wealth to be played there. Men walked with gougers tracing the line their narrow plows made straight as a die across the river. After them came the horse-drawn gougers cutting a deeper double furrow. Another army of men took up the game at right angles to the others, crisscrossing the wide fields. And then the sawyers came, slow with their loads of shoulder muscle and woolen shirts. They set in their saws and began the cutting of the gigantic checkers from the checkerboards on the hard Kennebec. The men stood to their work with both hands on the handles of their long tools, going down, coming back, fifty men keeping time as they ate into the stuff that meant their life, bed, and board, and fodder for their cattle. It was a sight to see the gates-ajar mustaches swinging like pendulums, gold and dark, and the breath in them changing to icicles as they worked. Every so often the picks spoke and the sawed lines lengthened ahead of the sawyers. Noon saw a dozen checkerboards marked out on the river. One notable fact about the tools of the ice industry on the Kennebec is this: they were the only tools that were good enough to remain unchanged from the beginning of the industry to the end of it.

Then the workers went to the shores and ate their cold ham and bread and broke the crystals at the top of the jugs and drank the sluggish milk. They built fires to toast their thick soles and sat on the leeward side chewing their quids of tobacco in the heat and haze of the smoke that made the tears run from their eyes. Fathers and sons broke into cakes and frosty doughnuts the wives and mothers had made. Apple pie with splinters of ice.

The afternoon saw the first great checkers of ice lifted from the checkerboards. With heaving of cant dogs and picks, the square crystals came up into the splendid

sunshine, sparkling like emeralds shading to azure in their
deep hearts, with sections of whole rainbows where the
edges were flawed. Layer on layer of brightness, layers of
solid winter to go into the hot heart of summer in faraway
cities and scorching lands. Long canals opened up into
dark water and men poled the cakes down to the ends,
where other men caught them with cant dogs as they
came, hoisted them up on the ice, slued them to the run-
ways. Chains clanked, the hooks bit into them, and up they
flashed along the high lines of steel and plunged into the
icehouses.

Inside, men caught the thundering cakes and switched
them, this one to the right, this to the left, to their places.
The walls of cakes rose gradually, aisles of air spaces left between the walls of solid crystal. The workers here were in
their shirt sleeves. They were the youngest of the men,
sons more often than fathers. Their work made them glow
inside like cook stoves. The sweat ran down their faces.
They stood by the cataracts of ice and flung the bright
streams each way, stepping as in a dance to keep clear of a
blow that would shatter their bones. The work was like the
thunder of summer in their ears, thunder all day long. And
the house filled up with the cakes. Square cakes piled as
even as the sides of a barn, true and deep blue in the
streaming dusk. The men walked between walls of Maine's
cold wealth.

And the steel-bright days went by. No thaws or rain
came to erase the grooves in the checkerboards. The icehouses were filled to their eaves and the last tier roofed in
the aisles between the cakes. Roughage was heaped over
all. The doors were closed and sealed.

That year the Hudson did not freeze over till March.
The betting of the Maine farmers had been three to one
against its doing so. They won their bets. The rival river,
the only rival the clear blue Kennebec had among the
rivers of Earth, had leankine stalls along its banks that year
of our Lord. The Lord had been good. The Kennebec ice
farmers heaped great towers of the harvest outside their
houses and covered them with spruce boughs and sawdust,
for extra measure. The Knickerbocker Ice Company lost
nothing, for they owned most of the icehouses along both

the Hudson and the Kennebec. All ice was ice to them.
The Kennebec crop was better than the Hudson, in fact,
for the water in the Maine river was clearer and purer.
Kennebec ice stood at the head of all ice. It was the Hudson ice cutters who lost. But if Peter was robbed, Paul was
paid. The Kennebec farmers went back to their hens and
heifers with wallets stuffing out of their trousers and their
sons' trousers, after the $4-a-week lodging and eating bills
had been paid. The grocers canceled whole tomes of
ledgers. The schoolteachers kept their patience right up to
"Horatius at the Bridge" in the Friday afternoon's speaking. New barrels of pork and flour came home to the high
farms on the whistling runners of the horse sleds. And barrels of halibuts' heads and brokenbread. Active Frost
stopped moving his checkers when his foreman turned to
take a shot at the spittoon. And Timothy Toothaker asked
the question when he brought his Susannah the first bunch
of mayflowers. They were married and setting up housekeeping on new pine floors and in the spooled maple bed
before the catkins were gone from the poppies.

The geese were coming back early, up along Merrymeeting, that same spring, before the middle of April.
And, in late April, that best day of all the spring on the
Kennebec came, when the first boat arrived, the Boston
steamer, with the star on her smokestack and her whistle
tied down all the way from Swan Island to the Cobbosseecontee, waking the dead and the hills with her news
of spring at last. There was not a church bell in the five
towns that wasn't ringing. Women in bombazine waved
handkerchiefs. School was let out for the day and the hills
were alive with children.

May saw the ice ships arrive and tie up at the docks.
The icehouses opened their doors. The Kennebec crystals
came down the runs, slithered across the decks of the four-
masters, and into the holds. When a number of the old
hulls were loaded, which had once breasted the waves on
the underside of the world, white under thunderclouds of
sail, a tugboat steamed down river on a neap tide, dragging
the old veterans of the Atlantic back to the Atlantic again,
below Popham.

And down in New York and Philadelphia, prosperous

citizens were getting down their ice-cream freezers. Children in Richmond and children under the shadow of the Blue Ridge were running starry-eyed behind high carts with letters frosted and dripping with icicles. The letters on those carts spelled Kennebec Ice. And deep in Alabama and Mississippi, pickaninnies ran with pieces of Maine's finest river in their black palms and heaven in their eyes. Farther south, the crystals of Maine touched the fruit of the Caribbees. Far down off the Horn and up the other side, ships with bones bred in Maine forests carried the Maine treasure to the Pacific. Trains plowed through the dusty cornlands of Nebraska and on to the Rockies, carrying Maine ice. and a whole nation knew the taste of the clear Kennebec. Half the world, too, England and France and Holland.

But all that was in the twilight days of wooden ships, when Maine women still kept their neat houses moving around the world. That was when the wizards had not wakened new secrets out of electricity and steel. That was in the eighties and nineties.

Now the Kennebec icehouses are rotting and falling back into the earth. Their interiors are taken over by the wasps and the mice. The old piers are sinking into the water. No ship comes up in tow of a tug through the first leaves of May. School keeps week after week and there are no bells ringing out to greet the steamer that leads up the spring. The gougers and saws are rusted away.

For the Kennebec crystals, last harvest of Maine's finest river, have joined the white pine and the spruce, the sturgeon and shad and salmon. The end is elegy. The day of natural ice is done. New men, outside New England, bring their sons in their strength to the work of refrigerating homes and factories. And the small farmhouses, back from the river, that once housed great numbers of young men and boys, are full of empty rooms where the swallows bring up their young, or they have only a few children who work at their tasks and never need turn their heads toward the river, where the strength of their fathers lay and their fathers' lives.

The other day, my good Kennebec friends whose, great house looks up the river and down, over a twelve-foot hedge of spruce, took me out and showed me the tools of the ice harvesters. They were dark with rust and covered with cobwebs. They had joined the flint arrows and the bows that once bent to bring life to the men along the ancient Kennebec. When we were coming back, we passed a strange depression in the woods, grown up with lusty spruces. It was the refrigerator men of my friend's house used a hundred fifty years ago. It was the ruins of the earth cellar where they had stored their vegetables in summer and winter, to keep them from heat and cold. It was the Kennebec refrigerator his ancestors and mine learned how to make from the Indians when they drove them away into the everlasting dark from the bright blue river. That refrigerator was ruin, and the Kennebec was as young and lusty as ever as it hurried toward the sea. Someday, our own sons' far great-grandchildren may find among the timbers of my friends's house the rusted shards of the electric refrigerator that serves the house today. And the Kennebec will be going down to the sea, as young and as fresh and blue as ever.

# 18  Uncle Tom
## and Tristram

Writers are good things to have in a family. The Kennebec family has had a good number of them.

The Abenakis, of course, were poets, being Indians, and though they did not write books, they made up poems and carried them in their heads and hearts—the best places to carry them—and when they needed them, in making love or putting babies to sleep, they had only to open their mouths and let them come. We have the love song that one Abenaki girl sang:

> Here I sit on this point whence I
>     can see the man whom I love:
> Our people think they can sever us,
>     but I shall see him while the world lasts.
> Here shall I remain in sight
>     of the one I love.

Most of the early navigators, Weymouth and Captain John Smith and the rest, could flourish a pen or had men who could do it for them. The river got into print early. Purchas wrote up the mouth of it. Father Râle was its first European author. He wrote an account of the natives, the Abenakis. Parson Bailey described the stream, its people, and the history that he helped to make. He soared into lyrics, too, and became the first Kennebec bard.

Brunswick was the birthplace of "the Boston bard," Robert Stevenson Coffin, and he passed eight years there, emigrating to become a printer. Between printing things

for the *Saturday Evening Post* and other parties and getting
captured by the British in the War of 1812, he turned out
miles of lyrics of his own. Among other romantic ladies, he
wrote of Melancholy:

> The moon is her lamp,
>         when the mist-mantled mountain
> At midnight she climbs, and walks on the steep;
>         Or leans on the rock of a crystalline fountain,
> And sighs to the zephyr that dimples the deep.

Perhaps the Androscoggin was responsible for some of
his fluency.

Bowdoin College, just to the south of Merrymeeting,
was a nest of singing birds. In one clutch of eggs, she
hatched Longfellow, Hawthorne, and John Abbott, in
1825. The music in the Kennebec Valley pines surely became a part of the singer of the "Psalm of Life." He spoke
of those whispering pines when he stood, a white-headed
old man, at his fiftieth anniversary of graduation from the
college, and cried his gladiator's cry, "*O morituri te
salutamus,*" into the face of the dark.

Nathaniel Hawthorne, who of all his great generation
of American authors remains the most alive and keeps his
place in the front rank of the world's greatest novelists,
wrote his first novel, *Fanshaw*, about his college town of
Brunswick while he was living in it. He drank and fished
the clear streams that flowed into the Kennebec and some
of the Colonial houses and Colonial minds of his tales
are surely Brunswick ones. He ran up the outside stairway
of one of the Colonial homes of "Back" Street as a red-
cheeked youth, none too easy a nestling for the academic
mother to keep under her wings. And J.S.C. Abbot, of the
same class, Brunswick born and bred, after trying his hand
at preaching and running a female seminary in the big
world, came home and took a house on Maine Street,
filled it full of his books, filled the state full of his books,
and the whole country. He wrote on the Austrian Empire,
on Russia, on Italy, on Spain, and the American Civil War,
and also on home and mother, the great Napoleon,

Napoleon III, American patriots, American pioneers, and
Frederick the Great. He covered a good part of the whole
world and a good share of its history. He well-nigh exhausted its store of great men. Fifty-four volumes in all he
had to his name. And all of them written "to make the inhabitants of this sad world more brotherly." He was one of
our first internationalists, yet he worshiped at the feet of
men who trampled nations like so much chaff.

The Kennebec may claim Anne Royall too, though she
knew it only as a visitor bent on spreading the light of
Unitarianism and her books—especially her books—along
the river. Anne was both Virginian and Unitarian, a combi-
nation hard to beat. She was also a teetotaler, a money-
maker, a traveler, a feminist, and a newspaperwoman. She
was the Nellie Bly and the Paul Pry of the early nineteenth
century. As editor of the Washington *Paul Pry,* she rushed
in where angels feared to tread. She tried for a long time
to get President Adams to express himself upon the subject
of intoxicating beverages. He was never at home when she
called at the White House. But Anne wormed out of some
underling the location of the president's swimming hole.
And when the president next day emerged from his dive,
he saw Mrs. Royall sitting on his clothes. She got her
interview. The president spoke with his chin rippling the
Potomac as he shivered and talked. Mrs. Royall was a de-
termined woman.

Her travels with the light took her into the darks of
Maine in 1823. She traveled up the Kennebec and she kept
an account of this journey and published it in her famous
*Black Book.* It was a black day for many along the river. She
set down the names of those benighted beings who did
not buy any of the books she was vending. The rich Mr.
Benjamin Vaughan of Hallowell was enshrined in her heart
forever and wore a halo in her book. For he, unlike most
householders, did not entertain the book agent on the
doorstep. He took her into his fine mansion, fed her "with
every delicacy," and slipped a banknote into her hands!
Anne wrote that he had an "illustrious eye" and a bow that
would have graced St. James's. She was all for him. And
she was all for almost everything in Hallowell. Even the

Baptist minister's wife and daughter were so charming that
she did not believe they had a spark of orthodoxy in them.
Anne was amazed to find a city in the woods of Maine of
such culture and book-buying propensities as Hallowell.
She was taken with the great houses and great ships and
the positive elegance of the citizens' living. It was a
wealthy place. And full of Unitarianism. Mr. Vaughan was a
bulwark of Unitarianism in America. And liked books. The
river was one after Anne's heart. "Kennebec," she writes,
"is principally settled by enlightened Unitarians and Uni-
versalists who carry souls in their    bodies." She went to
the Unitarian church. "It was the handsomest congregation I remember to have seen in any country; both men
and women were fine tall figures, fair and well featured,
with a nameless mixture of flitting graces and thronging
charms—the waving form, the sparkling eye, the glossy
curl, the jetty tufts of hair, the generous manly cheek, the
snowy forehead, the soft damask blush. But above all, the
kind glance of friendship and classic fire—it was impossible
to resist them."

That's the kind of people we raise on the Kennebec!

Augusta, though, wasn't like Hallowell at all. Anne
sold almost no books there. She was surprised to hear that
it was to be the seat of government of the new state. But,
then, it had been an orthodox town and nobody could expect much of it. If Anne Royall had had a vote, she would
have cast it for Hallowell, she wrote, where all the men
were gentlemen.

Another woman come to the Kennebec Valley later on.
And she stayed on for years, darning her husband's socks
and trying to keep some order and serenity among her
houseful of his children, at Brunswick. Her husband was a
man with a mission. He was the Collins professor of Natural and Revealed Religion at Bowdoin College, until the
money for the chair gave out, and he declared that, if the
college went on improving in morals for another twenty-
five years the way it was improving in his time, it would be
mighty close to whatever perfection a college could have
this side of the millennium. His wife went on darning. And
one day, when she was sitting in the pew of the First Parish

Congregational Church at communion service, she had a
vision, and joined Joan of Arc. She was a picture printed in
ineffable light like sunshine on a cloud. She was a venera-
ble negro dying after having been lashed by a slave driver.
The heavens were opened and a child looked down. The
woman got up from her pew in the midst of communion
and staggered home. She got quill and paper. She, too, had
a mission now. She wrote and wrote. When the children
got too ungodly obstreperous for her, she seized her growing manuscript and took refuge in one of the students'
dormitories at the college. A hundred young men were
preferable to a family in full cry. Her book was finished at
last. She could rest. It was published. It set the whole
country on fire. It was turned into a play and became the
only drama millions of Americans ever saw, the play most
often given in the whole of American history. Its villain
joined Genilon and Judas Iscariot, cracking his whip and
stroking his mustache among the immortals. Its kindly
black hero took his place beside Job and Tiresias. And its
little white heroine joined the angels in heaven. And a vast
war burst up into flames, which that Brunswick vision had
helped to start. And a hundred thousand young men
marched south or north into their graves across the middle
of the land. And John Brown's soul went marching on.
*Uncle Tom's Cabin* is the classic of the Kennebec country.
And Mrs. Harriet Beecher Stowe is the prophet.

There was another woman author on the Kennebec.
She never set a nation in flames with her books. But she
has written classics, too—classics which all the children of
the United States used to read and which some fortunate
ones do still. She is Laura Elizabeth Richards and her name
will live as long as Captain January lives, as long as children
like to read poems that are close to music and see windows
that are pure gold in the light of the setting sun.

Out in Casco Bay there is an island with a legendary
look about it. Half cliffs and half-high spruce woods that
send sharp points above the somber and mysterious shadows round their hearts, to catch the sky's brilliance,
Ragged Island is, next to my own Pond, the best of
Casco's jewels. This legendary land was taken by Edna St.

Vincent Millay. She was Maine's daughter before; she was
born beside the Penobscot, but Kennebec also can claim
her now that her harp weaves its song through the wind-
tuned Kennebec spruces. One of the great women poets of
all time, Edna Millay took themes from all the world for
her lyrics, which read as if they had always been written,
but the pith of her music is the clean strength of Maine.
The sharp loveliness of the evergreen sky line and the keen
light in some of her finest sonnets are the radiant beauty of
the Kennebec coast. Light calls to light: Edna Millay will
be at home, in her native splendor, among her jagged cliffs
and defiant, sky-seeking spruces. It is easy to see where this
poet got her mind that is built like a diamond. Maine
winds and winters and sudden springs cut the facets of that
fiery stone.

The Kennebec just missed two humorists by a few feet
of soil. But they were both born near enough the water-
shed, one to the east and one to the west, to be claimed
for the river. One was Artemus Ward, the first of the great
pioneers in the American art of laughter. He was born
Charles Farrar Browne, on a farm near Waterford. He went
west to grow up with the country as a printer, broke out
into humor in the Cleveland *Plain Dealer*, and finally
broke out into the whole nation and set it all laughing. He
became a "moral lecturer." He met Mark Twain in the
West and set him off. One of his best lectures was the
"Babes in the Wood," with the babes left out. He men-
tioned them, though, at the end: "They were good children, they were unfortunate, and, as far as I have been able
to ascertain, entirely respectable." He made America laugh
at a time when laughter was needed. Abraham Lincoln laid
down a tract of his, with tears in his eyes, to read the
*Emancipation Proclamation*. Artemus visited the Mor-
mons, and his lectures on the marital miracles of that set of
patriarchs made England burst her sides when he went
over there to his final triumphs.

The other humorist was Bill Nye. He was born on a
hardscrabble farm, too. A man born on a hill farm of interior Maine has to be a humorist to survive. Bill's family
emigrated to Wisconsin, to a 160-acre farm of ferns and

rattlesnakes, where, between Indian massacres, he attended school. His father finally got one glass window into his house before he died. Bill went west to Wyoming and became a newspaperman. He would have reported the Custer Massacre, but, as he said, he didn't get his trunk packed in time and missed the train. Newspapering set him off into laughter, too. He went east and worked for the *World*. He became a lecturer also, and his bald head and spectacles and long Yankee face probably saved thousands of people from getting discouraged about their own looks and helped them to go on living and become the builders of a great nation.

Bowdoin College has given Maine and the nation many authors.

For wherever there are good teachers there will be good writers. The number of scholarly books out of Brunswick is astoundingly large for so small a place. In my student days, there were President Hyde's books that make philosophy as exciting as life itself, and there were poems of Henry Johnson, one of the last of the great New England genus of professors of things in general, and his splendid translation of Dante. If I had to pick out one professor-writer of Bowdoin to represent all the rest, I might well pick Alpheus Spring Packard. He was graduated at Bowdoin and he taught there from 1824 to 1884 as professor of Greek and Latin, as professor of Natural and Revealed Religion, after Mr. Stowe's departure, and, during his last year, as acting president. He was probably the finest teacher Bowdoin, or any other small New England college, ever had. He found time to write many papers on educational and historical subjects. He fitted into the life of the town as first citizen of them all. And when he came to his time, he had the great good fortune to die at the edge of the sea, on one of the loveliest of the islands that fringe the Kennebec's mouth.

One of the greatest Kennebec authors was born in a white and sleepy village of the Kennebec country, at Head Tide, and grew up and went to school in Gardiner, on the Kennebec. When Edwin Arlington Robinson died, America lost one of the greatest poets she has produced. He

belongs to the world now, with Whitman and Dickinson
and Longfellow and Poe. He belonged to the Kennebec
Valley once. For it was in the big white mansions and the
little white farmhouses over which elms touch their wings
like guardian angles that E.A.R. first learned to know and
love and pity the men and women who have the shining
stuff of Tristram and Lancelot in them still, but who are
often wasted and lost on a world grown impersonal and
scientific and cold. The poet found himself there in the
lovely valley, a small boy whom two old New England
men, loving each other in a fierce taciturnity of the New
England masculine kind, used as their confessor at the
door of the sunset. It was here the poet found Aunt Imo-
gen, who could be tenderer as an aunt than a New England mother could be. It was here he found Richard Cory
and the Man Flammonde, aristocrats for whom the world
of today has no place. And it was along the falling piers of
Gardiner and Hallowell and in the abandoned houses of
the valley that he may have found some of the color of fu-
tility and air of decayed greatness that spread a solemn
shadow over his last long poems. Robinson, believer in
man and worshiper of life, was a man thwarted and discouraged by our progress without progression, in these
modern times. And surely the elegy of the empty Kennebec cradles, old houses and old towns with less life in
them than a century ago, left their mark with a peculiar
kind of eloquence on his fine mind.

It is something to have had the greatest Kennebec and
Maine author as a contemporary.

# 19  Yankees from the Province of Quebec

The English won.

The red soldiers with the straps making white crosses on them, front and rear, herded the Acadians like sheep into the boats. The ships rolled on the sky line. A child ran crying after her mother far away on the bay. A doll lay trampled and broken on the beach. Farther to the south, the cabins of Mt. Desert were blackened shells. The Castine homestead was only a cellar. The little Jesuit missions were heaps of stones that the junipers were covering. The dark-eyed French were pushed back from the coasts, pushed out of the cradle of the Kennebec; and golden-haired and blue-eyed young North Americans were being sung to by mothers and pines.

The years flowed by and strange, huge houses sprang up along the Kennebec and the Androscoggin wherever they turned white and came down over the granite rocks. They weren't churches, these houses, though they were full of hymns and the sound of great organs, and the services there brought men and women, and children, too, into them by the hundreds and thousands, more than in any churches. And the psalms sung there were psalms of life. Those who went in stayed all the morning and went back for all the long afternoon. There were no chairs in the houses. The blue-eyed people walked back and forth and thrust their hands among thousands of bright slender things whirling about. Vast belts came up from where the river roared through cramped channels in the dark, up through floor after floor to the top of the building. Vast

things with almost human intelligence handled threads
small as the spider's. A million threads ran out side by side,
keeping exquisite space between them. A million more ran
across them side by side over and under the others. They
swept out of sight through a wall. And in another room
they emerged as an entire thing, thin as the walls of a soap
bubble and white as driven snow. They swept into another
cave of Aladdin and came out long strips of white muslin
sprigged with rosebuds, rolled up and ready for women to
wear over wide wire hoops as they tossed their curls under
bonnets the size of a dollar and a sunshade that shaded
only a nose.

And one morning the blue-eyed people did not come
back to the church of the cotton. The men of them were
dressed in blue coats and trousers and wore a queer-stock-
ing-leg cap tipped over the left eye. There were drums and
fifes going. The women waved handkerchiefs and the
steam coaches pulled out of town with all the men singing:

> "Oh! Abraham Lincoln, what're you about?
> Stop up your head, or your brains'll run out."

And many of the men did not come back. Just dark
marks of them on flags full of queer holes that were
hung up in the hall of the statehouse at Augusta on the
Kennebec.

The mills started up again, after a little. But a change
had begun in them. The heads of hair among the spinning
bobbins were beginning to grow dark here and there. And
a very strange speech was under the hair, very quick, very
low down and high up at the same time, full of the lilt no
Yankee with a mustache would ever dare to have in his
voice. There were mustaches with that lilt, though, nice
wide ones with pointed ends.

The men of France were coming back to the Maine
their ancestors had left two centuries before. They were
following the white water down, following the Kennebec
and the Androscoggin. Each year they came closer to the
sea. The Yankees drew back from them, in the mills and on
the streets. But the men of P.Q. did not mind. They had

friends enough to keep them company. They kept coming
by new batches, cousins and cousins and cousins. They
wrote back home: "Big money down here, Uncle Amadis,
leave the farm. We work only fourteen hours a day here.
And on Sundays we wear our fine clothes and do nothing
but smoke. It is easy to learn, the weaving. *Sacre bleu*! It is
easy. You will get on. Of course, it is not home, not like
Canada. The people have not our ways. But there is the
money to think of. Even little Pierre has a pair of shoes.
Think of that!" And Amadis came along, wrinkled like an
old acorn in his face, and he prospered. He even got himself a cravat to his shirt. The Yankees drew back in the
towns. The houses by the mill piled up with P.Q. families.
Each year the line of Yankeedom retreated up the hill away
from the river. The blond heads were almost all gone from
the house of the organs of cotton. Stores began to have
two signs on their counters, and two clerks to each
counter, speaking two different tongues. Quebec and
Montreal newspapers appeared in the streets. Small Yankee
schoolboys shouted "Lard-eater!" on the lower streets and
they came home with black eyes. Every Kennebec and
Androscoggin city and town had its Frenchtown. Two nations kept apart, eating their different foods, having their
own ways, their own schools, their own barbers and bakers.
The French houses were poor ones, but they were crowded
full and ran over. Soon the better houses began to fill up
with the French. The sharp line crept uphill. One day there
were more French than Yankees in Waterville and Lewis-
ton. A Frenchman was on the Board of Aldermen and
smart French boys in school were learning "Snowbound"
faster than the Yankee boys.

It was a shame. Lard-eaters taking the bread out of
Yankee mouths. Foreigners. Why didn't they stay home
where they belonged?—Canucks! Frogs!—Foreigners.

But they weren't foreigners. Their ancestors had been
on the Maine coast as early as anybody's European ones.
Their ancestors had been in the Province of Quebec longer
than most Yankee ancestors had been in New England.
They were 300-year-old Americans.

And they weren't such bad people when you got to

know them. Of course, they put pomade on their mustaches and let their curls grow a bit too long for a man. They used their hands too much and seemed always on the verge of hysterics even when they were talking about the weather. Yet they had their points. They had kept, God only knows how, the old French idea that life every day is a little ceremony, with flourishes and gaiety. Gaiety! They had kept that through hundreds of years of lonely living in woodlands and small villages in cold, dark silences of winter nights, under mountains of ice and through winds like the winds between the stars. They had kept the French ideal of a home as a small hierarchy of graduated loyalties and balanced etiquettes in a howling wilderness where it was usually each man for himself and the survival of the strongest only. The most civilized of all the Europeans, the French, to whom conviviality and small gossip and the exchange of polite formulas of life, the village virtues, are more important than charters and bills of rights and bills of lading. They had plunged into the wildest possible lands of vast areas and enormous distances and lonesomeness like that of the mountains of the moon. And they had kept the village virtues of Old France in the New. Cut off from kindred, from currents of French politics, from all the stir of great cities, they had still remained Frenchmen. They had grown more so. They clung harder to kin and conviviality than the peasants of Normandy and the country of the Basques. They had dropped the frivolousness out of their conviviality and gained a lot there.

And they had added new virtues to the old ones. They had added a stern morality, which comes with hard life in hard climates, a deeper sense of religion. They were stauncher Catholics. Narrower of mind maybe, but deeper, too. They had grown to love their children with the same passion that the Yankees loved theirs to the south, because children were the only institutions, often, to keep their names alive, because children, and not money, meant old-age security, because their Quebec nation had its sole wealth in young husbands' strength and young wives' fertility. They had a lot of children because children were their inns, their towns, their religion. They could show the

Kennebec Yankees something in the size of families. A house? No. It was a little town. their bump of philoprogenitiveness, as my father, who dabbled in phrenology a bit and liked to read people's bumps now and then, would put it, was large. A home was every chair full and two in the cradle. Paterfamilias's old pants going down the ladder of smaller and smaller legs to ones the size of a good spank. Going to church was an army with banners, with father's wide mustaches leading a host. Meals were an endless chain of bowls with mother passing out the full and filling the returning empties. The Kennebec Yankees had slowed up. A man was rearing a family of eight and calling it a day. These quick, dark wiry men were keeping on to fourteen and fifteen and even to twenty, and not letting up even when winter snowed into their mustaches. They were coming into Maine as Maine people had gone into Wisconsin and Minnesota and Oregon. They were coming in with the vigor of pioneers.

The French Canadians gained a new strength the French of France had never had. That is the shadow of the forest. It was inevitable that the shadows of the trees under which they had lived all these hundreds of years should leave their mark. It showed in the cadences of their old songs and the way they could, on occasion, sink into an Indian quietness that was amazing. It was set off all the more by their old French gaiety. They had learned how to be alone and lonely. They were rather below average in height, but that wisdom they had learned under the northern lights and in lonesome cabins lifted them spiritually a head above their cousins in France. It made them kin to us, the Yankees. They, as we, had learned to live outdoors, under the sky and stars. They had been as quick as we were in learning from the Indians and going Indian in the woods. So they and the Yankees together ought to make a good start on a new kind of commonwealth.

The mill was only a milestone for these people. Even while many of the breed were working there indoors, their cousins were working outdoors among green pines and on white water, herding the forests down to the Kennebec sawmills. They formed a good part of the nation of

lumbermen. Paul Bunyan had a French-Canadian mother.
With eyes like huckleberries, I bet. They got on with the
outdoor Yankees from the first. They were never foreigners
in the woods. They made powerful friends. They knew axes
and they knew wood. They scraped their ax helves into the
shape of their own lithe and eager limbs. They talked to
their tools and they talked to the trees as people who un-
derstood one another. They loved work even more than
their blue-eyed friends. They went at the crosscut saws fit
to have the seams in their trousers make two of them.
They chopped and lifted themselves to a lather. I remember a Canadian lumberman of my boyhood who could take
up a barrel of flour in his teeth, lift one end of a loaded
hayrack, and do it all for the fun of it. He also taught me
how to make a sled, how to make a pipe out of an acorn,
and how to skin a raccoon the way you might take a child's
coat off over his head. I shall always love him.

  And now even the Frenchtown Canadians are moving
out into the country where they belong. They are taking
over the abandoned farms. Places where the Yankees had
to give up because their sons went away west and south, to
cities and new states. They have driven back the birches
and maples, repaired the stone walls, repainted the cupolas
of barns white, shingled and clapboarded and driven out
the swallows from the mows. A lot of Yankee bones must
be resting easier in their graves. The big old farmhouses
are the right size for them. They fill every room with a
child. They make friends with cows and hens all under the
same roof with them in the joined farm buildings. They
put up fir prongs to hang the tools on in the shed. They
have the organ in the parlor. They have the grindstone by
the grape arbor, where it belongs. They even join the
Grange. They work from crack of day to starlight. They
take pride in tall corn. They go to town Saturday nights.
They answer a visitor's question by asking another. They
are becoming Yankees fast. They even put the key under
the seashell on the front doorstep!

# 20 A Paradise for Fish

When I was on the sunny side of twelve, June meant
one thing to me. It meant a sky full of stars and a bay full
of them below, and my father sitting at the other end of a
boat with me, with his wide mustache like a golden fringe
in the lantern's light coming up from between his knees.
He was nothing but a half-seen well of light and a golden
fan of mustache. He sat quiet. I could hear strange watery
sounds around us, many feverish ones, quick and gone,
and every so often the under stars broke up into ripples.
Every so often, too, my father would rise up, shut off the
lantern's light from me, lean over and pull up a whole
length of fine crisscrosses of silver, pull them in and in, and
suddenly there would be a lovely wide slab of moonlight in
his two hands, thin as a knife at its edge, alive and curving
this way and that. My father would throw it down in the
boat among the other shad, and the fish would flap once
or twice, and choke into stillness with a wide, sad mouth
and eyes staring at nothing. Off at a distance there were
other lanterns floating between the stars above and below.
The bay was full of farmers turned shad fishermen for the
warm night's length, and the shad and porgies slapping the
water with their tails made music around them. I'd have to
work sleepy-eyed for hours next day, untangling our shad
net among the daisies of the field and picking the rockweed out of it. Never mind, the night of adventure was
worth it.

Any June night years ago, the Kennebec was laced
across with the corks of shad nets. You could see a dozen
boats out, up and down the river. Every farmer's wife

expected to put up her fifty jars of potted shad, and brown slabs of the Florida fish vacationing in Maine were a staple at table in early haying time. The hired men often swore they wouldn't be able to pull their shirts off at night, they had eaten so many shad the bones would stick out through their backs and catch in the flannel.

But June wasn't the only time that Kennebec men knocked off farm work to go fishing. They were on the best river, still, for fishing in the world. There was fishing at every season. In early spring it was smelts. They dipped them as they leaped up along the waterfalls of little brooks like slender arrows in the light of the April moon. They fried a lot of them right there, in the light of the moon, with pork chunks they had brought along when their wives had been looking the other way. Smelts were another ex-cuse for making a night of it. The spruce brush sent up its fragrant sparks that mingled with the stars and the men sat around it and smoked and told tall tales. And the boys sat up and took notice. But smelts were winter game also. Men fished for them through holes in the river ice. They sat for hours over the holes like pictures of Patience on the monument, and they piled their fish on the ice one by one. I can trace the decline of robust manhood in the evolution of the Kennebec smelt fishermen. In my boyhood it was just a buffalo coat and a hole, and the men's mustaches hung with icicles. Then it was a cracker box to sit on, then a lantern to keep their undersides warm. Then brush stuck up around to keep off the winds. Then the brush gave way to canvas. Now they sit in armchairs in a roofed house, heated by an oil stove and have a radio! So our manhood ebbs away! The men went after smelts in the fall, too, in a bigger way. They set out their loops of seines and pulled in cartloads of smelts, herring, bluefish, and jellyfish. They shoveled them out on the docks and sorted them over into big smelts and little smelts. They iced them from the farm icehouses for the train and Quincy Market and the brains of Boston. They saved the bigger herring. That is, we boys did. We strung them on sticks and carried them to the smokehouse. We lugged the popple wood and maple, and kept the fire going under them day after day. We would come out with fierce tears streaming from our eyes, get a breath or two of air, and go back to our smudge. I don't know what heaven smells like, but I have an idea. Maine bayberry will be mixed up in it, and the fragrance of the inside of a Kennebec smokehouse full of red herring.

Kennebec turkey! To me and any Kennebec man, those words are pure music. I know there is a Yankee joke in this name for herring. It is all of a piece with wind-pudding, which is a word for a dinner consisting of tightening the belt. But there is substance and truth behind the joke. For any Kennebec man would rather have a slab of that dark meat that grows in the sea than one off the best speckled and bearded bird that every blushed and gobbled on a Vermont hill. And herring is a foundation stone of Maine life and character.

There is a breed of Maine herring fatter and sweeter than this world-wide fish ever becomes anywhere else. It is the alewife. And you pronounce it "ell-y," in case you don't know. Alewives are bound up with the Indian culture. They were the fertilizer that made the miracle of milk without cows in an ear of the Indian grain. They swarm into Maine, in April, like bees. They come up the tidal rivers to spawn, in solid islands of silver. People dip them up by the trainload at Damariscotta. And dipnets are going all around the Kennebec's mouth, too. There were many in Captain John Smith's day, when the Indians fished them: "Their store of Herrings they compare to the haires of their heads." Where other fish have been exterminated by men's folly, alewives have survived in all their prodigal splendor to this day. There is no trout, making rainbows in fresh water, that can compare in delicacy with the taste of a fresh alewife. I know why so many fishermen clustered on Monhegan even before white men had been formally introduced to the New World. I know why the early settlers of Maine declared, "When others have prayers, we will have story and song." They had tasted the alewife. And the alewife is behind the twinkles in the Kennebec Yankee today.

There is no season when fish are out of season on the Kennebec. I had eeltraps in the summer and went after eels with stray uncles in the depth of winter. We had to sweep away the snow and cut a hole with the ax every so often in the ice of the marsh we were walking. Then my uncle would take his many-pronged dart and shove it home deep in the unfrozen mud below us. He would twitch his long mustache. "That feels good," he would say. I could tell by his mustache when he felt eels. And up he would snake them, two big yellowbellies, indignant at being brought up into the zero air from their snug mud, squirming between the barbed tines of the man's spear. Then my uncle would hand the weapon to me and let me pull up mine.

Fried eels are good, but smothered eels are better. King John went to his Maker after a dish of them. It was the right kind of end.

When Cap'n Cy Bibber gets on the subject of smothered eels, he lilts. They are his favorite fish. "My idea of a pretty way to die, is to eat so many of them smothered eels like Nance stews up that I'd die, anyway, and then have somebody shoot me over the empty dish!"

Of course, there are Cap'n Bibber's whales. Whales are beginning to come back to the Kennebec, now that lamps don't need to live on the fat of honest whales. Every summer, lately, they have appeared playfully among the coast fishermen. They were thick as fiddlers in Tophet in the Abenakis' time. The Indians went after them. They taught our ancestors how to go after them, too. They showed the men who were going to sire the great whaling men of Nantucket how to throw the iron into leviathan. Rosier, the historian of Weymouth's expedition, describes the way the Indians did it. They went out in flotillas of big canoes and surrounded John Henry Whale. The "bashaba," the chief bottle washer of the tribe, had the honor of giving the sea monster the iron. Only it wasn't an iron, but a former whale's rib sharpened up pretty, and made fast to it was a rope of tree fibers strong enough to hold John Henry when he got excited. His Royal Nonesuch was paddled up close enough so he could tickle the whale back of his fins. Then he gave him the works, the whale let out a bellow, and they all went away from there fast, whale, bashaba, and all the other red men, for they were all holding on to the rope, canoeful after canoeful. They went kiting, hell for leather over the ocean. The whale tacked this way and that, and some Indians bit the water, sudden. But the rest dug in their toes and held on. John Henry sounded, waving them all good-bye with his flukes. He went down "all afluking," as Kennebec men say of a horse or anything else that leaves them suddenly. He went down and stayed as long as he dared. But the rope held. He had to come up for air, at last. And there was the bashaba ready with a knife as long as your thigh bone and all his henchmen with their arrows on the string. They pin-cushioned poor Levi Whale with arrows and knives till he blew like a bursting boiler, turned over on his back, and waved farewell to the men with his little fins. It was a day. The Indians towed home their year's meat and cut it up on the beach, tried it out in kettles, and the papooses waded in sweetness to their little blueberry eyes.

Captain Smith, the admiral of New England, stopped off at Monhegan to hunt whales. He didn't get one. He said the whales weren't the best kind to catch, anyway. Sour grapes!

David Ingram, the walking wonder, mistook Monhegan Island for a whale. "I first took it for a whale, as those fish in that country are easily taken for islands at a distance, so high do their backs rear out of the sea, and so enormous are they that one would load a hundred ships." Let Izaak Walton match that for a fish story!

Hakluyt was as bad as Ingram: "There be seen some-times neere unto Island huge whales like unto mountains, which overturne ships, unless they be terrified, or beguiled with round and emptie vessels, which they delight to tosse up and down." Like Cap'n Cy's boat! "It sometimes falleth out that Mariners thinking these whales to be Ilands, and casting out ankers upon their backs, are often in danger of drowning."

And it was probably a Monhegan whale that St. Brendan landed on to celebrate Easter on his famous western trip. He thought it was an island. But he had hardly got his altar set up and a fire built to roast the lamb, when the whale got restless and started going, upsetting the whole ceremony of the first Easter service in the New World.

And the Unapieds are still there at the Kennebec's mouth. The Frenchman Cartier noticed them and gave them their name. The place seemed to be swarming with them. They were queer people, all right. They had only one leg apiece. But they got around spry in and out of the water. There's one island above Phippsburg that usually has a hundred on it even now. A gray grandad and all his harem. He has a full set of whiskers and he is the last to take to the water when two-footed people come too close. I don't suppose Unapieds are fish. The Greeks did not call them that, though their legs had grown together. They called them Mermen. Mermen wake people up along the lower Kennebec with their barking to this day. Seal is their common name.

There aren't so many cod as there were. They were thick enough to walk on once, by the old navigators' tell. The Kennebec codfish was a seal of the Old Kennebec patent, along with an anchor. It was really the foundation of our New England culture rather than Plymouth Rock. It saved the Pilgrims in 1622. A Venetian, Pasqualigo, with John Cabot in 1497, tells a pretty story to show how thick the codfish were on the Kennebec. He saw big bears sitting on the bank and fishing for them. The fish came up to snap at the leaves of trees and the bears caught them with their paws and tossed them ashore. But some of the cod were so big, said the Venetian, they pulled the bears in instead. That's the kind of codfish Kennebec raised.

There were lots of other fish, too. Weymouth reports, "plenty of salmon and other fishes of great bigness, good lobsters, rockfish, plaice, and lumps." The beauty of this Kennebec fishery was that freshwater and saltwater fish kept company. Thanks to the tides running up as far as forty miles, there were two universes of fish at every farm's foot. There used to be legions of bass. Weymouth saw great salmon jumping out of the river where Bath now stands. And there were sturgeons longer than a man. Sometimes they came right aboard the canoes when men were spearing them by torchlight, and upset the boat!

The Kennebec mouth was the Eden of fine shellfish. Lobsters were so plentiful that the early explorers caught them on hooks, according to Rosier. Even in my father's time, they came ashore in wind-rows on the islands after a sou'easter. Rosier describes the "great muscles," some of them with fifty pearls in them. And there were quahaugs galore. I once won a spelling match with that blessed shellfish. It was in New York State, and I was hard pressed. But my wife was giving out the words and she gave out this good Kennebec one. My friends and foes went down like ninepins. But it saved me, a Maine man. I won the match on it. I am thankful, though, that I didn't have to spell it the way the Algonkins pronounced it, "K'duquahock." It's bad enough as it is.

Most of the Kennebec fish are gone now. But they could come back if the cities would stop poisoning the river and give them a chance. And farmers could be fishermen again.

# 21  Whistling Wings

Doubtlessly God could have made a better berry than
the strawberry, said a seventeenth-century philosopher and
friend of Izaak Walton, but doubtlessly God never did. The
same applies to Merrymeeting among the bays famed for
duck shooting. There might have been better places to
shoot wild ducks in this wide green world, but they don't
exist, glory be to God!

One bright autumn day, when the maples suddenly
caught afire from inside and burned in soundless scarlet
flame all along the Maine coast, a whole army went duck
shooting. It was two hundred years and more ago, so the
soldiers were soldiers of King George. Their captain was a
Harvard man, grandson of one governor of Plymouth and
great-grandson of another. He took his soldiers out in
whaleboats and they rowed up and down where the ducks
made islands on the bay. It was a fine day, like crystal, the
kind of day Maine alone makes. The soldiers' business was
bigger game than that which came down in long arrows
through the sky. But this was a holiday and they were after
ducks. They shot plenty, until the whaleboats were car-
peted with them. The reverberations of their muskets went
echoing across the still water and up into the forest. There
was a sergeant along, by name of Harvey, and like all
sergeants he never knew when to stop. Young Captain
Josiah Winslow tried to keep the men in check. But there
is no moderation in sergeants. This sergeant pursued the
ducks he had winged close in to the shore. All at once,
muskets spoke from the trees and there came a yell to cur-
dle the blood. The duck hunters lost all interest in the
sport and three of them sagged over the gunwales. Then

the river came alive with slim birch canoes and devils with
horsetails for hair closed in on the whaleboats. Captain
Winslow turned back. The canoes sped down on him, too.
The soldiers sent back lead for lead. But the canoes closed
in. The Englishmen used their clubbed muskets on the
naked devils. All afternoon the fight went on. At dusk, the
captain's whaleboats got ashore. But the soldiers were
swarmed upon by new red bobcats. The captain was slain,
and every mother's son with him; twenty tall soldiers of
the king, with no grave ever to cover them. They had had
their happiness, though, before they died.

That probably is not the only time wars will be stopped
for the sake of duck shooting in Maine. Maine ducks are
worth stopping the best war in the world. And of all the
bays of my coast, Merrymeeting takes the cake for ducks.

When October rolls around, the year begins there.
Events around the bay are dated so many weeks and
months before the duck morning. A man's son was born,
for instance, on the third day after the law went off. He
cut his tenth tooth the second week of the next open time.
Every farmhouse in Dresden and Woolwich, Richmond
and Bowdoinham, is a garrison the night before the red-
letter day of the year. There is no thought of sleep. Boys
often, even, slip the apron strings and rebel. They sit up
with their fathers and big brothers. They eat slabs of cold
apple pie and pass rags and oil for the cleaning of the guns.
They suddenly feel their bifurcated nether clothes. They
take on the essential maleness. The rule of women is at an
end. They breathe in the thick smoke of pipes and drink in
the talk.

When the stars are at their highest and the cocks still in
the depths of sleep, all male Merrymeeting souls go out by
lantern light to the bay. The frost is pretty sure to be sifted
by this time. The men and boys walk through the dust of
diamonds. The last pale frostflowers crumble under their
feet. Pines loom larger than life among the stars.

Some people say that Merrymeeting Bay gets its name
from the meeting of the five rivers than unite to form this
sweet inland sea, the Kennebec, the Androscoggin, the
Abagadasset, the Cathance, and East River. The Atlantic

comes in, too, to lend its zest and spice, all the way up from Popham to Gardiner, at flood time. But any man will tell you that the name comes from the fact that the bay is one of the purlieus of paradise. It borders on Eden all the way, and a man can feel the breaths of the angels all over its blue waves. The five rivers wind into it through marshes where the tall grass furnishes enough cover for all the male habitants of the United States, from knee pants up to the trousers of the grandfather. Give every American male a shotgun, unlimited shells, and hipboots, and let them all loose there without women to complicate their days, and they would live in peace to the end of their time. They could return noontimes now and then, to propagate. But they would go right back again to the peaceful business of life. For wild rice grows all around the bay and all the ducks from the Western Hemisphere sooner or later come there to spoon up its grains from the water and give a man a chance at getting his living on the wing, as his ancestors did when men covered their nakedness with birds and lived in caves. Merrymeeting is a return to an ancient religion in which men send missiles up as prayers into the sky.

There is no farmer within fifty miles of Merrymeeting who is not a hunter when the leaves turn. A man may be the meanest of Yankees and slave all his life and slave-drive his woman and his children all the months but October and November. He may bury his money in an old-fashioned wallet under the stones of his pasture wall. But when the duck season comes, he digs out his silver dollars and moldy bills and gets himself cartridges and a twelve-gauge and goes after his share of the bay's harvest. For this is another crop that Kennebec men count on, along with alewives and smelts and potatoes and pumpkins—ducks and geese. For two months, all other business stops and men go down and wade and lie in wait, wet themselves to their skins, see dawn come up, run and fall, swim and sink and mire themselves, and rejoice like ancient strong men and like boys. Merrymeeting means renewing one's youth like the eagle's, the youth of man's days and of the race's.

The men and boys creep under the night to their chosen gunning floats and blinds. A Kennebec farmer's

stone walls may be so tumble-down that a two-weeks'
lamb can step through them, but he will work like a Trojan
and build himself a duck blind that is as fine a bit of
stonework as an old fort builder could ask for. His pumpkins may be choked down to the size of cucumbers by rag-
weed and smartweed, but he will have his house of brush
firm around him. His plow may rust, but his gunning float
will be shipshape and neat as a new pin.

The men stow their gear in the light of the lanterns
and they scull to their places under the stars. They untan-
gle the wooden tollers, masterpieces whittled from white
pine with a jackknife, the work of many loving hours  by
winter lamplight, which they have dug out from under the
hay in the barns. They rig anchors and set them out. The
subdued quacking of live decoys crackles around them.
The live ones are hitched to an anchor and put out in the
river, too. The men climb into their blinds and stow the
lanterns between their thighs. They smoke and tell stories
of fabulous hunts in other years, hold their guns ready and
wait for the dawn. Philosophy may come out of hiding at
such a zero hour, and men who are usually silent may put
into one sentence the art of getting along for a whole lifetime of good health.

The dark thins out at last. The air pinches up and
grows colder. A shrewd wind starts to blow from nowhere.
The plumes of grass begin to show up on the night. The
wind tapers off to nothing. The silence is all at once so
deep a man can hear his heart. Breaths quicken as they
come and go. The frost fog begins to flake and ascend.

A single gun goes off far away like a call to prayer. A
sudden arrow with all its barbs alive slants down through
the dark gray. The men throw their guns to their shoulders, wait till the ducks skim the water, and then turn into
volcanoes. Flash on flash of yellow fire, they give them the
left barrel, the right barrel, both barrels together. The boys
rise up on their haunches and let go, and come back after
each kick for more. The sound is deafening. The whole of
Merrymeeting Bay turns into an earthquake as the dawn
sweeps through the great pines. Guns roar, ducks squawk.
Sharp bodies hurtle over with taut wings that bite into

the air, flame jets, and the lovely wings that can think in
every feather crumple and shatter, and the arcs of flight are
broken. The wounded ducks strike the water on paths of
crystal, dive and go under.

Then the boats and the dogs put out. The bay grows
alive with men. Gunning floats slip past with boughs over
the bow and men blowing off steam behind. The whole
high sky is laced with chevrons of the risen fowl. The sun
strikes them while the bay is still only the gray of dawn.
The whistle of wild wings is a continuous treble music
between the bass chords of the guns.

And the hunters gather in their treasure, still warm and
resilient with life. They pick up the banquets they have
brought down, and hang them like chains about their
necks. The sun comes up above the pines like a vast bubble
of pitch on a Maine spruce tree. The men stagger home,
muddy and uncombed of hair and beard, their eyes like
burnt holes in a blanket. They walk half asleep. Their sons
totter beside them loaded with tollers, live and wooden.
The males go back to their farmhouses, a sight to make
she-folks weep. They carry hours of hard work and tens of
thousands of feathers that she-folks must pluck. But the
hunters have proved themselves men, they have got their
dinner in the ancient manner, and they keel over on beds
like lords of creation, like the gods they are.

Now that the rest of the nation has learned about the
taste of the Kennebec River that their fathers before them
had on their tongues in Kennebec ice, now that Maine has
become the holiday of most Americans, outlanders have
discovered the wild geese and ducks of Merrymeeting.
They come, too, now, in armies of khaki and brown flannel
and canvas. They come with dogs that have been lapped in
velvet and luxury. They come clean-shorn with the light of
prosperity and Wall Street in their jaws. They come with
guns that are machines for raking all the horizons with destruction. They come spruce and neat  and polished, and
unbelieving. And after one night on Merrymeeting, they
are blood brothers of the men of the Kennebec. They
come back unshaven and dirty and coarse. And they have
turned back five thousand stale years of indoor living. They

have fallen in love with the stars and running waters, with maple trees and the white dawn, in the only right way for men to fall in love with them, by being out among them and drinking them in through the skin. They come home with a life redder in them for the strength and wonder of the Kennebec.

This is one crop the Kennebec still raises. Manhood that is rooted in hunting. Feasting that whistles on wings.

# 22 Cap'n Bibber's Coot

All Cy Bibber's boys have their guns, of course. Cy supplies them, in turn, out of his arsenal, as soon as each son gets heavy enough to stand up behind the kick of a man-sized gun. They can take the kick remarkably early. Some of them are not as long as the shotguns when they first get them.

And, of course, Cy does some shooting himself. Nothing to speak of; nothing to take him from his work. Oh, he gets his allowance of ducks in season, but that is in the early morning hours taken out of sleep. Cy hasn't really taken a day off to go gunning since he was nine years old. That's what he says—nine years old. He takes a gun along with him in his boat when he is seining, in case a sheldrake or wild goose should get sassy or attack him. And he carries a gun when he cuts his winter wood, for fear a rabbit might bother him. But all this is in the line of duty. It doesn't count as real gunning.

One of Cy's boys told me about the time his father got his famous coot. Cy was going to town, on an October morning, with a cartload of smelts to ship. A stray coot came right down close and low and bothered him. Cap'n Bibber pulled his twelve-gauge out and let him have it. The horse was taken by surprise and gave a sudden leap and threw Cy out into the road. But Cy never noticed the horse. That coot was winged all right. He was so full of lead that he bounced him on every spruce as he went over. Cy had to put him out of his misery. So he took after him.

The horse, by some miracle, having run his fright out of him, turned square around in the narrow wood road, load and all, and went back home. The upper pasture bars

bothered him some, but he got through, and most of the
cart, though the smelts were left right there. Mrs. Bibber
unharnessed the horse from what was left of his rigging. It
was seven o'clock in the morning. Cy had got an early
start.

Mrs. Bibber and the boys heard shooting all day. Now
it was in the north. Then it swung round more to the
west. It came from the suth'ard, out near the Atlantic, at
last. It sounded like a whole battery in action. It covered a
lot of territory.

At sundown, the boys discovered the smelts, hitched
up the horse and took them to town in the second-best
cart.

Just after sunset time, when they were putting the
horse up, they heard their father coming. They went out to
see what he had got.

He had got the coot. One little lone bird, and not a
shell left to his name. He had torn his town pants in three
places. He had spoiled a good pair of army shoes. He had
ripped his coat on a barbed-wire fence. But he had his
bird.

When they tried to eat what was left after the feathers
had been taken off, they bit into almost pure lead. That little coot must have weighed all of eight pounds. Mrs. Bibber said it had covered the kitchen table with shot.

The boys always called that bird "dad's forty-mile
coot." He had been about that far to get it. And had
blown away $1.56 in shells. But it wasn't what Cap'n Bib-
ber would call a day's gunning. No, sir!

# 23 Folk on the Farm

A Kennebec farm is an unmistakable thing. It has a lean to it, first of all, and trees and plow horses are trained to shorten up on one side. It isn't so bad as Paul Bunyan's crew getting to be longer-legged to port than starboard from cutting a mountain section, but something like that. For no matter what way you go, you have to go uphill or down. And that gets into living there. There are no dead level days.

"I tell Nance," says Cy Bibber, "She has to give me plenty of room in my underflannels fore and aft, I have to hinge up so much getting them potatoes in the upper patch. Molly, she's used to working on an upgrade, poor cow, she can mow among them junipers good's a goat."

You notice another thing right off. There's always water tools mixed in with the land ones. You have to back an eelspear out through the mowing machine wheels before you can start haying. The bagged Baldwins in the shed are mixed in with the split and dried hake, open ledgers of the life of the sea. The horse hoe is mixed up with wicker eelpots. The shingling hatchet and hammer are usually in a clam rocker. Like as not, there is no room in the woodshed for wood because a reach boat fills up the whole place, lifting the sheer beauty of her high bow toward the rafters. And the shavings around her mean so many unpulled turnips and unthreshed beans. But they also mean life more beautiful than turnips or beans can ever make it. When you split the chunks of beech, you have to be careful not to leave your ax hung in a loop of warp with a lobster buoy hanging to it. Outside, it's the same story. The cow's milk in September may taste of tar, because she's been

grazing where the seine was spread out after going
through the tar kettle. A Kennebec farm is an amphibious
affair.

There's another funny thing. There are tollers lying
around everywhere, wooden ducks sitting on bunches of
shingles for mending the leak in the barn. And guns lean in
the corner of the kitchen along with the brooms and mops.
The tollers are the local idea of a duck. They are whittled
out by hand. There are lots of whittled things around—the
weather vane, hooks for the children's coats, the butter pat
with the acorns on it. You might get the idea that the
farmer here hasn't put away childish things, like a jackknife
or a rifle or toy ducks.

Until lately, there was usually an old uncle or so
around who had been to sea. He presided at the sawhorse
in the woodshed, most often, but his mind was in other
places and you felt that the broad timber of his back and
thighs was being wasted on work a boy could do. He usually ended up by getting a boy to do it. There were plenty
of boys around handy in those days. And the uncle sat on
his broad beam and told the boys about the ports he had
seen and the ships he had helped handle and worked the
boy to such a lather of excitement that he just ate through
the spruce. It was a fair division of labor and the boy
thought he'd got the better of the bargain. The uncle was
the kind of man who had a shaggy mustache and shaggier
eyebrows, and he squinted. He squinted because he had
used his eyes as three-diameter field glasses for years along
the coast or off on the wide Atlantic. He had hair in his
ears to keep the wind out. He kept the hair on his head
clipped short. His hands were wide because he had handled a lot of halibut in his time. He could use the roundest
cuss words as a boy can, with innocence in his eyes. He
had twinges of rheumatism here and there, but he could
get around spry. He smoked a pipe that could knock a
common man down. He did not chew, like the boy's father. He didn't know much about women. He had been
too busy with boats. He kept himself young, and all the
people on the farm. The schooner he had rigged up in a
Jamaica-gin bottle the boy took to bed with him, and the

boy had the intaglio of the bottle in his ribs when he woke up in the morning.

A peculiar kind of aunt is still a feature of the Kennebec farms. She is usually more a purge than provender. She did not marry and she did not want to. Men are too easygoing things for her. She has picked so many huckleberries on granite ledges that she has rubbed a lot of the stone into her. She is very necessary to have around on a Maine farm, for the other people on it otherwise might get to thinking that work is too much like play. She usually wears spectacles and she has read the Boston *Transcript* since its beginning. There is no call either for Sunday school or church around where she is; she takes the place of both. Of course, she is a living limb of the old Puritan spirit. She works hand in glove with the Maine winter to keep people hard. So cuss words are silenced in her presence and any very open gestures of love or affection have to be kept out of her sight in the farmhouse. She is one of the reasons the old sea uncle used to like the woodshed so much.

The children on a Kennebec farm are a bit peculiar, too. Somehow or other they never have any idle time on their hands. They don't sit back and wonder what to do next. They run from one thing to another. They have a fishpole at the end of the bean row and a house made in a bull spruce near the strawberry bed. They sleep out there every now and then. They insist on staying up late, even though their trousers are no longer than a good ear of corn. They go out and stay with their father when he is after a treed raccoon. They have so much fun running around, they run around a potato patch picking off potato bugs without knowing it is work.

The women, too. They have to work by the light of the morning star at the kitchen window more often than any other women alive. They have to carry more pails of water. They often pitch hay as well as milk cows. They even climb trees if the turkeys break out on a tear and take to the branches. They have many rooms to keep in apple-pie, New England order, but they are out picking strawberries, blueberries, raspberries, blackberries, huckleberries, and cranberries half the time. They are a calendar of all the summer months. You can tell by their pail or basket what moon or what berry it is. And they put them all up. And they put up all kinds of fish, too. They put up everything going. For half their year is frost and snow. And yet they find a lot of time to be with their children. And their husbands. That is even queerer. Usually farmers' wives get as far away from their men, and the men from them, as they can. Sometimes a thousand-acre wheatfield, even, does not satisfy them. But along the Kennebec it's different. The women seem to want to be with the men and help them in their work. They even take hold of one end of a seine sometimes, or one end of a crosscut saw.

I suppose the typical Kennebec farm is small. Maybe only sixty or seventy-five acres. But, all the same, it has a lot on it. It has more different varieties of loveliness called trees than any other farm on Earth. Pines, spruces, hemlocks, three kinds of fir—but also popples to make running water with their leaves, among the quieter oaks and maples and beeches and hackmatacks. It has many kinds of crops. All the way from apples and barley to sassafras and smelts and spruce gum. It is furrow and forest, and even more ledges. It has sand and clay, cockleshells, clamshells, the side of a mountain, a brook or two, the bank of a river, or a bay, and stones of all the assorted sizes in Christendom. And it also runs over into all the other farms, up and down the river. Like the old Abenakis, Maine farmers look on all lands as a common hunting and fishing ground. When they are after a three-pronged buck, they get it, even if they have to corral it in somebody's orchard ten farms away.

The farm raises a few cows, a horse, a few chickens, turkeys, maybe, ducks, geese, stones—they actually do breed on a Maine farm—dogs, cats, pigs, sheep, tame crows, and bright-eyed boys and girls, tougher than the roots of a pasture juniper. It is diversified farming. But not so much of any one thing is raised for the thing to become a burden.

One day I was walking along the Cathance Road and came on a farmer getting in his hay. There wasn't much of it to get in. The Christmas trees had crowded in too close and the orange and lemon hawkweed had pretty well crowded out what grass there was. But the man was good and hot. He was raking and bunching and pitching on and stowing and treading all at the same time. He was also carrying a three-year-old, very tight in his short pants, piggyback most of the time. He could pitch on a good forkful even with the boy around his neck. And there were two more, bigger boys, on the rack. They were making-believe tread, but I noticed the farmer had to get in and go over the load with his big feet every so often. The farmer had gray in his hair, as well as hayseed. He must have been in the fifties. But he was still smart enough to have children. He sweat as much over playing with the children as he did over his work. I couldn't help thinking there was something all Maine about the whole picture. The wild evergreen woods, the small hayfield, the one-horse outfit, a farmer able to play with his young ones right in the middle of his work.

"Pretty good load you've got there," I said to him.

"Yes," said the farmer, throwing the three-year-old son up on the soft hay on the rack so that he landed broadside up, "about as good a load as a man could ask for, when they grow up and fill out their clothes."

It occurred to me that he was speaking of the children.

The old Kennebec Valley could be a pretty good cradle still.

# 24 A Patchwork Quilt

After all is said and done, the best crop a river can raise is a civilization. And civilization means not only fine houses and cities and great men, but also good cookery, good stories, a great many bright proverbs, and a touch of the super-natural. It means human beings, and human beings who have put their roots down into a place and have grown to be first cousins to its clouds and trees. The Kennebec Valley is rich in folklore and human nature.

You can tell a lot about the people in a place by the proverbs they have made up out of the whole cloth of experience. If they have had a hard time, so much the better for their adages. Their wise sayings will sparkle with wit and irony. If they have gone down to the sea in ships, the poetry of sails and winds will be in them. If the folk idioms and proverbs are sharp and homely, and full of beauty too, then you can be sure the makers of them have lived in a hard and homely and beautiful place. It is like a proposition in chemistry. You can be certain that such sayings have come from somewhere around the Kennebec.

Proverbs are not merely decorations on life. They have life itself in them. They are the bedrock substance of living, built up by many people and many years. They are the beginnings of all literature, the first metaphors and similes, the first comedies and tragedies. They are the first poetry we have. The Kennebec Valley is rich in such poetry, a poetry of Yankeedom; tart, sparkling, and full of meat. There are some Kennebec people who are "small potatoes and few in a hill." There are some with "faces only a mother could love," they are "homely as a stump fence," they are "homely as a basket of eels," and their faces look like "a

plum duff with an acorn thrown at it." There are a great
many who have top-lofty notions, they are "nasty-nice"
and "butter wouldn't melt in their mouths," they are "independent as a hog on ice," they are the "white hen's
chickens," "proud as Lucifer," they go with "head up and
tail over the dashboard," they need to "have the wind
taken out of their sails." There are some folks who would
"break the heart of a grindstone," some who "can't see a
hole through a ladder." Some people are "eyeservants" and
some "no more use than a trimmed nightie." Some
women "bring their pigs to a poor market" when they
marry, some live on "wind-pudding." Some folks are "cold
as slow molasses," some are "dead as doornails" and "sit
like bumps on a log." There are some who are hanging on
by the "skin of their teeth," they are ready to "kick the
bucket," and have "one foot in the graveyard and the
other all butter." Some folks are so saving that they are
"too mean to die." But there are others who are a "sight
for sore eyes," and "bright as a silver dollar," and "smart as
a cricket," and can do a thing "in two shakes of a lamb's
tail." Some are "poor as Job's turkey" and "laugh out of
the other corner of their mouth." There are a good many
mean people, ones who "pinch a cent till the eagle
squeals." Some have "as many faces as the town clock" and
are "slippery as an eel." Some have "the Old Boy in them
in the stink of onions," the "Old Boy in them bigger than
a woodchuck." A man may come in to a scanty dinner, but
"a short horse is soon curried." It often "rains pitchforks."
The rain sounds "like sheep droppings hitting on a shingle." A bad boy gets it laid on "till his eyeballs jingle."
Some men "tread on their wings" to every woman they
meet. The winter wind blows around the eaves and cries,
"no pork and no molasses!" Some people always "get the
wrong pig by the ear." A man has to work to "keep his
mouth from growing over." The mosquitoes are often
"thicker than fiddlers in Tophet." Things are right when
they are all "shipshape and Bristol fashion." And "many a
little chip makes up a ship." So books of wisdom are made
up, and the psalms of life.

Cap'n Cy Bibber lets out a proverb almost every time
he opens his mouth. Only he doesn't know it, and that's

the beauty of it. He makes up poems as he talks. His friend
Jerry Prince had a pasture in which his cows dried up. But
it was good gravel and now Jerry has feathered his nest by
selling it to the road makers, and Cap'n Cy calls it "Jerry
Prince's diamonds." Cap'n Cy had a rooster that was
wabblecropped and no use as a breeder. Cap'n Cy said the
bird "didn't have no authority," and he "was no more use
than last year's crow's nest."

Good cooking is the universal sign of a civilization. If
you can find a place where smelts are baked with pork
scraps crisscrossing them into a sheet of golden eloquence
that makes man forget his taxes are due, then you are in
the midst of culture. The only real baked beans in Christendom never got south of the Kennebec. I shan't tell
what goes into the pot besides beans, because I think
the Kennebec has done enough for America already. Our
smothered eels are no dish to be sneezed at. Baked raccoon is no poor-man's meat. Nor are skates' fins. Lucul-
lus's mouth would water at them. We cook a deep apple
pie in an iron skillet, with pork in it, that is a whole banquet in itself. And we have a chicken soup, with the whole
chicken in it, and dumplings that are like thin sheets of
the Promised Land. They are native things of which the
foreign macaroni is a poor mockery. We have cod-lead
dumplings, too, for sinkers in stouter stews, named for
their shape, not their weight. We have hogshead cheese
and calves-head cheese that beats the Pennsylvania Dutch.
We used to have hulled corn that was as near heaven as
maize could come. The Kennebec cods-head chowder can
renew anybody's taste in life. And our flapjacks outdo the
most aristocratic of southern waffles. They can, as Cap'n
Bibber says, put whiskers on a man's feet. If you haven't
eaten venison grilled over Maine spruce boughs in the
frosty Maine air, then you have not started living. We have
pies, of course, of all the New England varieties. But no
pie on Earth can come within a hundred miles of a Maine
blueberry one with the spice and the sunshine of Maine
boiling over its edges in the oven. And there is no real
piecrust south of Portsmouth. By the test of cookery,
Maine stands at the head of the nation.

The Kennebec region has had bigwigs enough, such as

every civilization has. Indian chief in beaver and swan
plumes, a noble Frenchman turned noble savage, a homemade baronet, a Jesuit martyr, Yankee martyrs who died
defending their wheat and their sons, a Tory preacher, an
Amazon Kennebec queen, a Maine Odysseus, a woman
with a book in her that fired a nation, a governor who
started barefoot, great captains of the seven seas. The Kennebec had statesmen, James G. Blaine, who just missed the
White House, and Thomas B. Reed, one of the wittiest
and most eloquent of men ever to stand in the halls of
Congress, who embalmed the stupid flies who opposed
him in the liquid amber of his remarks. And the Kennebec
was visited by other bigwigs. Arnold used it as a highway,
Talleyrand was brought up in Maine and fell into Maine
brooks, Lafayette was entertained on the river, presidents
and admirals came here, and Marie Antoinette was invited
to come but missed the boat, and the beautiful house furnished for her remained empty.

But smaller people have left even more eloquent
memorials of human history. There is the woman buried
with a stake driven down through her ribs, for taking her
own life, at the crossroads in Brunswick. There is Hunter's
Tavern in Topsham, where the ragged Continental soldier
came to lodge and found the place so pleasant that he said
he would stay all his life. It got to be awkward for the
widow who took him in, for she wanted to stop keeping a
tavern. But the old soldier swore he would stay "as long as
a single shingle remained on the roof." He kept his word.
He stayed on alone, after the widow went elsewhere to
serve her grog to the men going to meeting in the old
East Meetinghouse, to wet their whistles for the psalm
singing and fill themselves with fire for the preaching.
There are a thousand and one such men built for an epic.
There was the man who would not tell what he wanted at
the table. "Tell by my face what I want!" he would shout.
And his wife would run out and fetch the vinegar cruet.
There was the man who made his wife get up from the
table every so often, go out and run around the house to
keep her supple. He would make her catch his horse and
then set the horse loose again, and make her do it all over.

Masterful men who were bound the world should know
who wore the breeches in their house. There is that item in
the book of the Brunswick watch, that makes the old life
seem kin to our own: "March 4th. One thing is deserving
of particular notice, viz., not a hundred rods distant a fine
lady was observed to be sitting in the lap of a fine gentle-
man, and as our respected major and squire would say, 'all
as fine as silk.' Past twelve of the clock, and a fine and
frosty night!"

There are stories enough along the Kennebec Valley to
make up a whole book of ballads. There was the bear that
Granny Young killed with a paddle when coming home
from blackberrying on Bomazeen Island. There is the story
of Mr. Stover's hearing squeals from his pigs and going out
and finding a huge bear holding a pig in his paws like a
sandwich and taking nibbles out of it. Mrs. Thomas, walking to Brunswick from Harpswell with her new baby and
half a quintal of fish, was pursued by wolves at Middle Bay,
but she threw a fish out every so often for them to fight
over. She arrived in Brunswick with nothing but Ephraim
Thomas, a future citizen, left in her arms. It was a lucky
catch of fish. Samuel Stanwood saved his dinner in his pail
and it saved his life when wolves attacked him at Mair
Brook. He gave it to the wolves that surrounded him and
he went home from there under full sail. He got home just
ahead of the wolves and screamed to his wife to open the
door. She did. And he got in one jump ahead and banged
the door to on the wolves' noses. The howling of wolves
was heard in houses on Maine Street in Brunswick by people living just yesterday. The loup-cerviers were worse than
the wolves, and lasted longer. The Maine folks pronounced
them Lucy-V's. They were big wildcats. They made the
woods hideous at night with their cries. They might attack
a man. One man had scars on his back that he said were
put there by a loup-cervier that jumped his back on the
way home one night. All his neighbors, though, said the
man had fallen down a quarry when he was coming home
with a skinful of whisky in him. Lucy-V or whisky, he had
the scars, all right.

One of the best tales is the saga of Isaiah Winter. Isaiah

stood six-three and had a beard that brushed his front
pants. He was of the timber of the patriarchs. He had
raised three different complete sets of children by three different wives. And there were other children of his running
the woods and hills, too, folks said as knew. He was a hard
man on his women. He was hard on men, too. He asked
and gave no odds. He took what he wanted. He wanted
the field adjoining him on the north and he moved his
fence over and took it. The widow there came out and
pleaded with him, but the fence went over. She had no
money to go to the law. Isaiah hated soft people. He did
not go to church. He was an atheist. But he believed in the
devil. Folks said he had seen him the night his last wife
died. She had worked herself to death for him, and he
wouldn't send for a doctor. Neighbors brought one too
late. Silas Trufant saw something big and black stamping
around back of Isaiah's barn, when he started home that
night. It had eyes like two big balls of fire. It was something vast. It was breaking down the rails in the bull pen.
But Isaiah didn't turn over a new leaf. He got himself a
housekeeper and carried on with her scandalous till his last
children left him.

    And one night when Isaiah was walking late in his
woods, a loup-cervier jumped down out of one of his trees
and tore his coat off his back and clawed his body to ribbons. Isaiah fought him off, but he got marked for life.
One big scar from his forehead to his beard that looked
like the finger marks of a giant's hand. That loup-cervier
left his sign on him. It was the only thing that ever mas-
tered Isaiah.

    Isaiah swore a great oath, before a lot of men, that he
would get that wildcat. He bought a gun and he hunted
him day and night. That cat took him so he neglected his
crops. He got himself some bear traps and set them
around. People did not dare to walk in his woods, for fear.
He set poison baits and Luke Simpson's coon hound ate
one of them and came home and died on his own
doorstep. But Isaiah did not bag that loup-cervier. He
grew worse as the years went by. Isaiah kept hunting for
the beast. People were all talking about Isaiah Winter's

lion. It was a great joke. Men would laugh about the beast in the grocery store. But they would give Isaiah's woods a wide berth when they went past at night. Somebody said he had seen the varmint. That is, its eyes. They were like big balls of fire. And the man heard crashing in the woods, too. Isaiah let his farm go all to seed. His housekeeper left him at last, and took up with a younger man. She told tales to make your hair stand on end. How Isaiah would sit in the dark of his house and swear awful to himself for hours, sit by the open window, with his gun across his knees, looking out at the moonlight and waiting for the loup-cervier to come.

He went kind of crazy, at the end. Stayed out in the woods for night after night. People heard him hallooing. An old man hallooing is not a good sound to hear. They saw him with his old beard full of moonfire. And one night they heard a yelling that made their blood run cold. In the morning they found Isaiah dead in his wood road. His throat was all torn away under his white beard. And on the other side of his face from the old scar there was a new one—a mark of a great row of nails, from his hair to his beard. Isaiah Winter had found his lion.

But there are other tests by which to tell a civilization besides proverbs and stories. Superstitions are a pretty good sign. The Kennebec people have some old ones and some very pretty ones. Of course, there are lots that have to do with the flood and ebb of the tides. People do not begin things on the ebb, if they can help it. Neap tides figure a lot in family histories, as courtings often come to a point with them. There's the old belief, on the lower river, that dying people will sometimes put off going until the flood slacks off and the tide begins to ebb. Very small boys may sometimes be kept truthful for fear of having their mouths sewn up by the devil-darning needles—which other places know as dragonflies—if they tell lies. I know I was. And if a girl out blueberrying looks into a freckle lily, she will catch a batch of freckles if she doesn't know how to take care of herself and say the proper rhymes. Cat-nine-tails are not to be brought way into the house, but put in a

jar on the shelf in the side entry. That's far enough for a
wild thing like a cat-nine-tail to go, unless a housewife is
looking for trouble. Popple is an unlucky wood to go in a
ship or a house, because the wood of the Cross was made
of it. And that's why the leaves of the popple have shivered
ever since.

The Kennebec has a phantom ship as good as any that
ever chilled a sailor's heart. She was built in Freeport. But
she will never return there. She used to come slanting in
past the Kennebec's mouth in the old days of sail. All her
sails set and full, coming in with a fine bone in her mouth.
But there never was a mother's son seen on her decks.
Never a sign of life. And she never got home.

> ... Never comes the ship to port,
>      Howe'er the breeze may be;
> Just when she nears the waiting shore
>      She drifts again out to sea...
>
> In vain o'er Harpswell Neck the star
>      of evening guides her in;
> In vain for her the lamps are lit
>      Within thy tower, Seguin!

And just as sure as she came in sight, in a few days the
funeral boat would be going over the water to the graveyard islands with four men at the oars and the mourners in
the stern. For the phantom-ship's coming meant death to
someone. Many old people along the Kennebec can recall
walking down, as boys and girls, to see ship launchings,
taking part in the last scene of an epic of American history,
in the twilight of the gods of wood and sail.

There was a house of religion in the region. On the
Androscoggin River, before it joins the Kennebec, there
is the vast ruin of the Holy Ghost and Us château of the
Shilohites. The place was built by men and women who
followed in the footsteps of a man called Elijah. He was
only a plain schoolteacher, but he had a vision, and in the
vision he discovered that he was the old prophet reincar-
nated to redeem a sinful world. He set out preaching. The

millennium was at hand. Hundreds of men and women,
hungry for an Apocalyptic radiance, left all and followed
him. They climbed the hill of Shiloh and built the great
house where, in twin towers, a man and a woman, relieved
like sentries, knelt perpetually at prayer. They sent out
apostles, two by two. They built a great yacht, the *Coronet*,
to sail in, on pilgrimages to the Holy Land. But evil days
came. Elijah was sentenced to life in prison in Atlanta for
causing the death of one of the Shilohites. The colony dis-
persed. But in late years some members came back. They
held forth in the ruining house of prayer. They saw a
solemn warning in the flood of 1936 and they said the
time was not long before a universal one. And Elijah, freed
from Atlanta, is lying somewhere hid, ready to claim his
kingdom when the hour strikes.

There are pleasant bits of color to make up the patch-
work of the Kennebec's folk quilt. There are winter bou-
quets that have to do for half the year in the land where
the brier rose must be brief. There's cat-nine-tails and the
waxy everlasting roses with spots of gold at their hearts.
There's the loveliest bouquet of all, marsh rosemary,
picked in the tide's way, with purple stars stitched on it
that last through the months of snow.

The lore of homemade remedies still flourishes in the
houses back from the main roads. Sassafras tea and pennyroyal tea, good for most of the ills of man, and yarrow,
witchbroomed in the attic to keep illness away, good for all
the ills that pennyroyal does not cure. I once had an herbal
aunt, as most Kennebec people had. She smelled of all the
pungencies of a Maine pasture and a cold that could resist
her was a man-sized one. One remedy there is, peculiar to
the heart of Maine, I hope. That is the laxative nanny-
plum tea. You find nanny plums where the sheep have
marched on their narrow track through the ferns. It is,
they say, efficacious. But my aunt never went that far in her
pharmaceutical frenzies. My mother used goose grease on
us children, though, and camphor bags tied on strings
around our necks.

There are corncob dolls with husk dresses and beads
for eyes. There are ship models of every craft that ever

sailed the seas. Full-rigged ones. Every house has some. But the finest and most typical art form of Maine is the half-hull ship, built out of strips, that once served as an actual model for some great ship that went down the ways into the Kennebec. The lines and curves of these are the best kind of symphony there is to go over a mantelpiece.

There are whittled objects everywhere round in houses and barns. For the Maine winters are long and Yankee men are great men with a jackknife. Of course, there are the hooked rugs, with hens on them as stiff and proud as hens are in a real barnyard. And there are the scrolls of braided rugs that spread the spirals of life all over the best floors of Kennebec houses. Spirals made out of dresses and trousers worn there and turned now into beauty after a career of usefulness. Crazy quilts are monuments to all the gowns and glory of generations of women in a home. Homemade art still lingers by the river.

Not all the patches in the Kennebec quilt are bright ones. There are the little red mittens a father found by the rift in the river ice below Richmond, to keep as a memorial to his little lost daughter. There are the bones found bleaching among the pussy willows of the riverbanks when the spring freshets have gone down. Men and children are taken by the floods. There are other ruins, too. Fertile farms left dunes of blowing sand. The skeletons of fine bridges crushed and shattered. The Great Flood of 1936 left one span of the Richmond-Dresden bridge in the middle of the river and one half buried on Swan Island. Houses and barns went down the yellow highroad to doom. But that flood had its lighter moments, too. A baby was born upstairs in a house after the waters had filled the lower story. He and his mother were taken out through the window into a launch. The proud French-Canadian father called the new son Moses!

# 25 The Kennebec Phantom

It sounds queer to the landlubber, the way seafaring men sometimes talk of ships. As if ships were people. In the heyday of Kennebec sails, there were vessels whose names have a ringing sound in Maine history like queens' names—Boadicea and Elizabeth—in the chronicles of the English race. And now and then you hear of a ship that was as a woman born to disaster. Such was the *Arethusa*, lingering to this day in Kennebec mythology, the phantom annunciator of death. Like Mary of Scotland, in her end was her beginning. A dark glory from a weird and evil sky covered her brief life from the day she put to sea under a woman's curse till her embers were scattered on the water.

She is not the only ship turned ghost in Kennebec folklore. She could not be, for too many hulls slipped down the river freighted with splendid dreams and manned by youths reared on Kennebec farms, who were ignorant of the sea's ways and the strangeness of Eastern ports and eager for them.

What is a phantom and why is it? The question is a bone of contention among the metaphysicians, and one of the stone walls between them and the materialists. Where the scientists fail of a wholly satisfying answer, a poet's guess may serve its turn. So perhaps the phantoms that stand for an instant in the Kennebec's mouth, with tenuous sails, like thin clouds, are the eager desires, the fantasies, of youth shaped by primitive intensity into images no harsh impact of actuality could shatter. Reappearing at intervals out of the night, or the dawn, or the fog, they

189

float on the endless mystery of the sea to this river of elemental and fiery dreamers.

Yes, there are good tales of ghost ships, and well told. But the legend of the *Arethusa* has several points of special interest. For one thing, it is not a straight-away story of linking parts like, say, the wreck of the *Hesperus*. This is a broken tale, with bits of it strewn along the river, hither and yon, and it has been a task to pick them up and piece the puzzle together. I suspect that there are fragments that belong to other Maine myths and I feel very sure that other fragments are there because some old sea captain read Homer. Many of them did; the *Odyssey* was natural reading for them.

For another thing, there was the woman, lovelorn and bitter against the man who turned his prow away from her, and whose curse brought the horror upon every mother's son of the *Arethusa*'s crew. She is only a misty shape, nameless, nothing is known of her and, apparently, nothing has been imagined. Yet she will not go down, because she is practically unique: it has never been the habit of the tall sons of the Kennebec to allow women power to affect the destiny of ships or of men. Adam on the Kennebec knows woman as Eve, the lost rib that returns to him to restore his strength. His idealism pictures her as normal and clear and steadfast in her subservient place, the helpmeet. And his idealism, no less than his pride, would be offended by the alien concept of a woman cursing the man she had plighted troth with and having the power of doom over him, his vessel, and all aboard. So, in a way, it isn't odd that I couldn't discover any facts about the woman who turned the stars in their courses against Jael Merryman and his ship *Arethusa*. Kennebec men wouldn't want to talk about a woman like that, they wouldn't want to know much about her; they'd want to wipe her out of mind, they'd want to forget her very name. So would their women. And it is forgotten; I couldn't find it. I don't believe she was a Kennebec girl. A woman like that must have come from someplace else.

Everything, so the tale goes, went wrong with the *Arethusa* from the start. Right off, there was her name. Some seafolk believe that names beginning with "A" are

unlucky. It's all right for a man to be called Aaron or
Alexander, but if you're a sailor and your wife was chris-
tened Annie, call her Nancy and take off the bad luck. The
same with ships' names, nothing beginning with "A."

When Aaron Merryman said he was going to call his
ship the *Arethusa*, everybody warned him, but he wouldn't
listen. Stiff as a steeple, he was; a churchgoing man who
wouldn't allow any idolatrous superstitions; a stubborn
man you couldn't tell anything.

Aaron had never really followed the sea himself, but he
must have his ship like everyone else. It was a mystery
where he got that name for her, they said. It isn't a Maine
name. Aaron was bookish as well as pious; and they believed he got it out of some book. Then he gave the
*Arethusa* to his son, Jael, to captain; a young man just into
his twenties and with no real experience of the sea. Maybe
Aaron, not Jael, broke off the match, and this was his way,
putting two or three years of time and the width of the
globe between his son and the girl. Of course, Jael had
made a couple of trips to Rio—who hadn't? And Aaron
sent him out as master of the *Arethusa* to roll the seven
seas to ports on the other side of the world. Loaded him
up with pine lumber for Java. Gave him a fine crew. Most
of them were young men, but not all. There was one about
forty, Dan Thomas, the mate. But, as I've said, most of
them were young, strong with youth and eager with
dreams that had grown up in them with the slow, hard
yield of the fields they had helped seed and harvest from
childhood, dreams that had caught a bold, piercing brightness from the crystal river and the sharp blue edge of the
sea. From the tales of seamen, these saltwater farm lads
had woven a dream fabric more magical than Aladdin's,
blended as it was with the deeper, primitive magic of
Maine.

There on the other side of the world, they knew, lay
the East, blossoming and sweet-smelling under the earth's
shadow, like a garden patch of sweet william and
mignonette sending up fragrance through their way
against wind and wave, to see at last with their eyes all the
wonders they had seen already so vividly with their minds.

So the *Arethusa* set sail laden with dreams, youth in

the rigging, and young Jael Merryman for master. Apparently no one but Dan Thomas, the forty-year-old mate, took any note of the wraithlike figure on the wharf crying curses into the wind.

I had picked up a bit of the story some years ago, as it had come from Dan Thomas. My informant, an old sea captain, had grown up on a farm hard by the shipyard where Dan Thomas worked. Dan Thomas was over sixty then, and he had long quit the sea. This is the gist of what he told, as it came to me from the old seaman who had been a lad, barely in his teens, when he heard it.

They had trouble from the time they crossed the line. The ship's carpenter fell from the main royals and broke his brains out on the deck. On a perfectly calm day, when there was no motion to the ship. That was an odd thing, his falling like that. He never had dizzy spells. He was steady as a church spire. After that, it came in gales. They had to fight for every inch of headway clear to the Horn.

It was summer down there, but big blows were brewing. The wind was all over the lot and the clouds were piling up miles deep. The air felt wrong. Dan Thomas told afterwards how night after night the masts dripped with St. Elmo's fire. He had never seen such fire in thirty-five years of sailing. There were balls of it, big as lanterns, burning blue, and awful to look at in the dark. Night after night. They could almost hear it hiss, Dan said. It got on the men's minds.

Then it was albatrosses. Never so many seen at one time before by sailors! All at once, scores of them came out of nowhere and flocked around. One or two lonely ones would be natural. But not scores. They came down close, too. They flew right beside the men as they worked in the yards. They touched them with the tips of their wings. That's an awfully bad sign, any seaman will tell you, to be touched by an albatross's wing. It bothered them to no end. A sailor killed one of the birds with his clasp knife. Reached out and cut its throat as it flew alongside him. Captain Jael told the men to shoot them. He entered the wingspread of each albatross in the log. There was one nine feet seven inches long, from wing tip to wing tip, Dan Thomas said.

Bad weather dogged them up the Pacific. It caught up with them at latitude thirty. It came in a gale that made their eyeteeth rattle. The hurricane sails were ripped to ribbons. They rolled three days with bare poles. The *Arethusa* lost her foremast and two good men. Stove flat, they were, and sucked over the side like so many jackstraws. They were the lucky ones, along with the carpenter—the way things turned out.

The gale blew itself out at last. Then the doldrums hit them. They stuck to the glassy sea till they began to foul up along their water line. Three weeks of doldrums. The heat ate into them. The tar tried out and bubbled at the seams in the deck. The sails hung like dead things.

They got a wind at last. And the lightning held off for a time. They put in at the Sandwich Isles, I think it was, and got fruit and water. Two of the men quit the ship there; and Captain Jael took on six natives, being so short-handed. "Monkey men" had been Dan Thomas's name for them, and he didn't think they were Sandwich Islanders. They brought some kind of drug along, and they got a lot of the men to chewing it. Maine men, brought up on honest tobacco to chew! It did something to them. Jim Moody, who wouldn't hurt a fly back in Maine, whipped out his knife and cut one of the monkey men almost in two. Then he stabbed a white man, one of his next-door neighbors back home. Jael was blazing mad about that. He put Jim in irons. The white man got well. But the dark one went over the side.

They reached Java after a while. They unloaded their pine at Batavia. Dan Thomas said Captain Jael got terribly taken in by the Dutch dealers. Anyway, he would ship no cargo there. He left in a high dudgeon and went skirting Java eastward, like a cork on the water, and no cargo to hold him down.

Here, I think, is where Homer takes up the tale, though the narrator is still supposed to be Dan Thomas of Maine, mate on the *Arethusa*.

It was a coast like a boxful of jewels. Mountains of turquoises went up sheer and turned into heaps of pearls where the snow hung on them at their tops. At the foot of the mountains it was all emeralds. Showers were coming

along all the time and they dragged rainbow after rainbow
over the hills. There were birds there flying, like beads with
a fire burning inside of them. It didn't seem real to anybody. The Yankees had been around a lot, but they had
never laid eyes on any place as shining as that one was.
They could look deep down into the water under their keel
and see strange, huge fish swimming far under them like
the mermaids the old-time sailor-men used to see. The
clouds in the sky were odd shapes, too, and they filled up
the blue with temples of snow. They could smell a strong
scent of millions of flowers, coming to them off the land.
Nights, it was even stranger. The dark came down like a
black waterfall, all at once. Then it was big stars and big
fireflies, till the air was full of lights and they couldn't tell
where the fireflies stopped and the stars began. It was just
as if they were lying all the time in the haze at the foot of a
rainbow, and the crew got to seeing things no plain sailing
men ever saw before: especially the young men who had
sailed from the Kennebec full of dreams, leaving behind
every solid thing in their lives.

They came to a deep harbor under a mountain and all
hands went ashore. Jael led them. He was the first to jump
into a boat. Not a man stayed aboard the *Arethusa*. They
all rowed ashore and the young men sang.

They rowed up abreast of a little village under palm
trees. And girls with big blossoms in their flowing hair
came singing and swimming out to meet them, naked as
fish in the waves.

Then Jael stood up in the boat. It seemed as though
something snapped in him. He plunged into the sea and all
the young men followed him. The strange women lured
them on through the water to the shore and the thick,
scented foliage. Lovely it was, at the time. Lotus Land,
Nepenthe, Circe's porcine craft, singing Sirens, and not an
ounce of beeswax in any man's ears.

How many days it went on after that, none would remember. They lost track of everything, lying in the soft
grass, lying in flowers taller than they were. They ate now
and then, but did not ever remember what it was. It was
the women the *Arethusa* men remembered, and their eyes

with no expression in them, like the eyes of heifers. Not like women's eyes. The women were laughing all the time. And there was always that drowsy sickish-sweet smell. Jael lay on the grass with all the rest. He wasn't different from them. He was like one of them.

Then, Dan said, they began to find dead men. One day—some day or other—they saw the first one. He had a beard on him now, as they all had. He was lying by the beach and the whole back of his head was gone, and what was left was swarming with flies. Somebody tried to cover him up with sand. The rest just sat around with their hands hanging limp from their knees. They all must have wondered a little, though, about the man's head. Maybe they thought he had got some kind of fall, an accident. His name was Will Hacker. He was twenty years old, big and powerful, and he had a young wife at home, a true Kennebec girl who never cursed a man.

Another day, there were two more beards pointing up to the sun. One the bodies had an odd kind of spearhead, bound round with grass, sticking out between its bluish ribs in front. The man's chin was bent in, as though he was still looking down at the thing. The women with heifers' eyes came out of the woods with fresh flowers in their hair.

It was about then Dan Thomas found himself running and dragging young Jael Merryman with him. Jael struggled; he didn't want to go. There were others of the crew running, too. The women were coming after them, with their hair all flying with flowers. One caught up with Dan and tried to pull Jael away from him. He flung her off and ran on, dragging Jael.

The women splashed around them as they slid their boat into the water. They had to hit them on the fingers to make them let go of the gunwales. There were some other men of the crew back under the palms. The women held them around their arms and legs. And dusky short men came up behind them as they struggled and ran long spears through them. The men in the boat could hear the screams.

They reached the *Arethusa* somehow, climbed aboard, and got up enough sail to make a start. They put in at

some port in the Pacific islands and took on natives to help
them. They headed for home. But the nightmare hung
round them even when they were across the Pacific. And
there was that queer smell on them.

Jael kept to his cabin most of the time, and Dan
Thomas sailed the ship. Jael seemed hardest hit. But the
others did not worry about him. He had started it all.
They blamed him and hated him; remembering their dead
mates and the screams under the palms. Once, when they
were nearly down at the Horn, somebody took particular
notice of Jael when he was walking on deck one day. He
had one arm bandaged. And the fingers sticking out of the
bandage were as white as chalk.

They stayed away from him.

The nightmare did not lift even when the Atlantic
wind blew cold around them. Nothing seemed able to
blow away the odor that clung to them.

They had raised the Maine coast and Seguin was
showing at the jib boom, and the Maine sun was going
down, when it happened.

Jael Merryman came out of his cabin with his two
hands white as chalk raised before him. And the whole
place behind him was fire. Jael was laughing loud.

"I have cleaned the *Arethusa* now, and it will be all
right when we get home." They say that was what Jael
said, and then he began to laugh again.

It was too late to do anything. They all got away from
the Arethusa in the boat. They watched her burn as they
rowed toward dark Seguin. The flames stood up white
where her sails had been. She was all gone by the time they
grounded their keel on Small Point, by starlight.

They agreed among themselves, before they separated
that night, never to tell enough about what had happened
to bother people. They made up a story that would do.

For months nobody thought there was anything
strange about that story. They didn't even talk much about
the fact that young Captain Merryman was very sick up in
his father's house, and no one could see him. They weren't
surprised that Aaron shut his door on callers: he was never
a man to make folks feel neighborly. They let him alone.

Nobody but his father ever saw Jael Merryman again. Even
the undertaker didn't see him, it leaked out afterward.
Aaron nailed his son in his coffin.

This fragment of the *Arethusa*'s story is not taken from
the Odyssey; which inspired Dan Thomas, or more likely a
seagoing man of higher rank and culture, to merge in one
episode the singing Sirens, Circe turning naive men into
swine, and the land of the Lotus-Eaters. Whatever adven-
tures befell the men of the *Arethusa*'s crew in the magical
maze of the Eastern islands, there is no doubt that young
Jael Merryman came home a leper. He must have told
things to his father before he died. Aaron would want to
know why he had burned the *Arethusa* and all the capital
he had put into the building of her. He'd have to know
about that. Jael must have told him the true story that
wasn't out of Homer. But Aaron never said a word, and
nobody asked him. If Aaron was a man you couldn't tell
anything to, he was one you couldn't pry into, either. It
aged him, people said. At fifty he looked nearer seventy,
and he was more strait-laced and pious than he had been
before. It might be said that he gripped himself to the
walls of the little white church on the sea-facing hill, like a
barnacle to a rock. And he hung there, gripping his rock of
ages; silent and alone. Aaron wasn't ever a man people
liked.

Two or three of the men who had quit in Eastern
ports, or at the Sandwich Islands, came back later in other
ships; and they and the young men who had landed safely
off the burning *Arethusa* took to the plow again. For several years, anyway, none of them went to sea; just a trip,
maybe, in a fishing schooner, but they didn't keep on with
it, and they never said why they were passing up the good
money in fish and the free life of the sea. People didn't
think much about it; they could understand how the shock
of the whole thing, the ship burning and Jael dying, might
take the edge off seagoing for them for a while. If they saw
one of them looking seaward with strained eyes and a
quiver to his nostrils, as if he watched for a shape on the
horizon and smelled a scent on the breeze, they didn't
comment on it nor wonder about it. They were sane

Kennebec folk with their feet solidly on the ground and
their heads held level in the wind, knowing only natural
fears and sorrows; whose youthful dreams had not been
snatched from their normal place, in the heart, and made
visible in shapes of weirdness and horror.

Then Lem Goodnow, one of the *Arethusa*'s crew, decided to go in for codfishing on the Banks. He was around
thirty by this time and had a good wife and several sturdy
young ones. Lem had hardly got out of the Kennebec's
mouth before he turned around and came home. No reason at all that anyone could see! And Lem never gave any,
except that he had changed his mind. He sold his schooner
and went back to farming.

One day Dan Thomas found out the reason. Maybe
because Dan was not a youth but a mature man, with several long voyages behind him when he shipped as Jael's
mate, he hadn't taken the *Arethusa* affair so hard as some
of the lads. He had been fishing out between the Kennebec and the Banks several years now, and coming home
with nothing more to report than good catches, which was
probably why Lem Goodnow dared to try it. Dan Thomas
was just starting out of the mouth of the Kennebec one
afternoon, bound for mackerel, when he met the reason
why Lem had turned back.

It was a fine clear afternoon. There was no chance to
confuse things. Dan looked up and there it was. It was
coming in from the ocean to meet him. It had every white
sail set. It was coming, and coming fast. And there wasn't a
soul on the decks. Not a mother's son of a sailor anywhere.
It came flying down on him. It was going to hit him fair. It
was the *Arethusa*.

Dan Thomas said his men told him afterward that he
screamed and screamed. They held him by the shoulders
and the arms. They said he kept on screaming about white
hands. That was all. He didn't scream about anything else
but that. And after a bit he threw up both arms and
stopped screaming and waited quiet as a lamb.

He was waiting for the sound of the *Arethusa*'s boom
in his sails. But it never came. When he let his arms fall and
looked again, there was nothing but the empty Atlantic
ahead of him.

But Dan Thomas's sailing days were over. He got a job in the shipyards the rest of his time. It was there my old friend got to know him. And noticed his queer trick of not looking at people he was talking to; and the way he used to smell of his hands sometimes when he thought nobody had eyes on him.

The men who sailed in the *Arethusa* were not the only ones ever to see her phantom sails. She has appeared since their time. Lem Goodnow and Dan Thomas did not die immediately after seeing her. The death legend may have grown up later from the coincidence of her appearance and the passing of some person of importance in the community. But this is one of the lost pieces of the story that I have not traced. Forewarner of death, *Arethusa* lingers yet. And it is not fog nor the moon that projects her. She comes in the clear sunlight. Look for her, fisherfolk say, on a May morning, when the day and the year are young.

# 26 Cap'n Bibber Philosophizes

The kitchen window was open for the first time of the year. There was a slender shaving of a new moon clean as one of Cap'n Bibber's white-pine ones right in the middle of the square opening. The thin pipings of a hundred peepers in Cap'n Bibber's culvert were coming through the open window, too. It was a mild April night. But Cap'n Bibber wasn't missing his regular evening consolation, warm weather or not. He was sitting at the stove with his stocking feet in the oven. There was a nice fire of spruce going, and the sparks and smell of it came out through the open grate. I thought I smelled wool singeing and told Cap'n Cy I thought he had too hot a fire and was scorching his socks. He said, no, good wool always smelt that way. Guess he'd be the first to know if his own toes were catching fire. He threw in another chunk of spruce. A man needed heat in his feet and up his pant legs after a good day's work, winter or summer. He shifted his corncob, leaned back, and rocked.

Cy was a great rocker. He went all around his kitchen floor evenings in his rocking chair, when he was resting. Just as soon as he'd bring up at the wall, he'd get up with his chair held right smack to him where it belonged, go over to the middle of the room, plank himself down, and begin all over. He liked to rock all the wrinkles out of his mind, he said. It was good for a man to rock. Half the trouble in this country was that men didn't use a rocking chair any more. He would go back and forth across the kitchen to prove his point. But he was anchored tonight.

His feet being in the oven held him fast. He would work up close to the stove, but every so often he'd hitch himself back and start over. The rocking helped circulate the heat up his legs, Cap'n Cy said.

There was a good smell in the kitchen besides the spruce burning. I'd know that smell among a thousand. I swung round. Sure enough, there they were. A bunch of mayflowers in a kitchen cup that had the handle knocked off it.

"Mrs. Bibber been mayflowering?"

"Well—er—no," said Cap'n Bibber. "I picked them mayflowers." He blushed red as a beet. "You see, it was this way. I never bother about no highty-tighty things like going flowering. But I was taking the brush off that dory of mine this afternoon down in the swale by the cove, and them mayflowers was so thick underfoot I had to pick a lot of them to keep from mashing them up. You know how it is. A man don't want to mash things up. Not even mayflowers. I just happened to pick 'em. Women like things like that."

"Yes, I know," I said.

"Guess they hanker for flowers," Cap'n Bibber went on, "way we men might hanker for a nice string of frankforts. Me, I'd rather have the frankforts any day in the week!"

"The mayflowers smell good, though," I allowed.

"Yep. They smell like spring. Sure sign of spring, better'n wild geese. I used to go mayflowering when I was a boy. Guess we all did. My boys do."

"All the boys abed?" The old mince-pie clock said only eight. But the house was still enough to hear a pin drop.

"All but Bill. He's still out. Say, do you know?"— Cap'n Cy leaned toward me confidentially over the arm of his rocker, and the twinkles came at the corners of his eyes—"I believe that scalawag of a son of mine is up to diving in tonight head over heels."

"Diving in?"

"Yes. He's been thicker'n thieves all spring with Hen Bailey's second girl—that spunky one with the red hair and full of mischief. I shouldn't wonder if Bill up and asked her

this very night to keep house with him this summer. He's
been an awful long time brushing himself up tonight, and
he went out of here in his best pair of pants. That's a good
sign. And he took most of the mayflowers I got down at
the cove right along with him, too, when he thought I
wan't looking. Them flowers you see ain't a circumstance
to the bunch I picked. Bill's got the most of them. So I
guess I've picked mayflowers for more women that just my
Nance. Yes, sir, when a boy man-grown takes a fistful of
mayflowers with him, you can bet your bottom dollar
something's in the wind. Shouldn't wonder if I was a
grandaddy by mayflower time next year. Bill's a smart boy.
And a good one. He wouldn't have no trouble keeping a
family in potatoes. And a boy can't start too young being a
man. I started pretty young myself. And I hope the first
young one is a he-one."

"What's the matter with she-ones, Cap'n Cy?"

"Oh, she-ones are all right. But they're blanks. They're
all right in the house, but a man wants to have somebody
to help him in a boat, with ropes and traps and tar. And no
girl's up to that. It's nice enough to have a girl after you've
got your boat hands attended to and a good working crew.
Say the sixth or seventh one. That one might be a she. To
keep her mother company and man the house. I never happened to have one. Nance is kind of sorry, I guess. But
there's no ordering Providence. I know some men who've
got nothing but a mess of girls, and see how sorry they
are, out in their reach boats all alone. Nobody to give
them a hand on an anchor. Too bad!"

"But there has to be just as many women as men,
Cap'n Bibber. What'd your Bill and your Tom and your
Frank and the rest do if there weren't any wives when they
grew up and needed them?"

"Oh, there'd always be plenty girls, all right. Them
white-collared fellers in the towns would breed 'em, and
there's always the fellers on the coast who can't seem to
get anything else. Farmers and fishing people need boys.
They used to have plenty, too, and their boys stayed at
home where they belonged, in them old times. They didn't
get to thinking they was better than their fathers, before

them and go off to the towns and get jobs where they
wouldn't get dirt on their hands and could wear their
Sunday-go-to-meeting clothes every day in the week. They
stayed put.

"That's the trouble with our country nowadays. People
don't stay put. The ones along the Kennebec do, most of
them. But they are a mighty small drop in a big bucket.
And they were getting to running around too much, too,
with their new buzz buggies and all. A man oughtn't get
much farther from home than a horse can take him, or a
yoke of steers. It means something to sleep in the room his
grandaddy slept in and look out and see the old people's
graves under the locusts inside their white fence. Home
ain't just where a man washes up and eats and sleeps.
Home is old trees that has grown up with a man from the
time he was only knee-high to a grasshopper. Home is
where you know the mayflowers will come up sure as rain
every spring of the year, right in the same place. I picked
my first bunch right there where I picked Nance that
bunch today. And now I've picked Bill's. Kind of a circle."

The captain did not say anything more for a long time.
There was only the silvery sound of the peepers coming in
from the night outside. And the clock ticking on. At last
the captain knocked the ashes out of his pipe.

"Home is roots. Same as with a tree. A good pine has
got used to his ledges and knows where to go to find the
water with his taproot. A man has to take hold of his land
hard and grow into it. And shape his body to it. If he
wants to feel good and be a first-class man. A man wants
to fit into a bay and know where the shoals are and the
bold water. Wants to own his own boat and take care of
his own things. Things he knows. Things he's got used to.
That's home.

"Half the trouble with people now is they don't have
no home. They've got away from the land. They've got
away from the water. They want to have their wheat raised
for them by factory hands. Want to have their fish caught
that way. The farms out west are factories. And the fishermen who go out of Boston and Gloucester are hired men.
Hired by the day. They don't own the tubs they sail. Why,

they was a sardine sloop down here last winter, and all the
men did was play cards and wonder when they could strike
for more pay. They never talked about no sardines. They
just talked about getting back to Boston and going to the
movies. City fellers—that's all they was. Didn't have no
pride in their boat. She was dirty as a dunghill. They didn't
own her. They was just tenants. That's what coast fishing is
coming to. A lot of hired men!"

Cap'n Bibber spat into the woodbox. His voice got
deep and his mustache trembled. I never saw him so stirred
up from the bottom before.

"Hired men—the lot of them!—Fishing ain't just fish.
It's catching the fish and running the boat that's yours,
just as much as the two hands you have. It's a man's pride
and gumption, and doing the whole business by himself.
Farming ain't just plowing or running a machine. It ain't
just turnips or beans. It's opening the earth up to the sun.
It's putting in the seeds by the handful. Feeling seeds with
your hands. Putting the heat of your hands into your
seeds. And it's seeing the green things come up like
crooked baby fingers and then slendering out. Farming is
hoeing and weeding by hand. And picking your beans and
threshing them with a flail your father made and swung before you was born or thought of. When you was just the
ground he was working in and fine corn coming up for
him with its yeller hair in the wind. When you was the
strength and life he was looking for in the earth. When you
was back there, the other side of his body, in the wind and
the rain. That's what farming is. I guess it's good as religion. It's a kind of religion, when you come right down to
it. Religion."

I had never known Cap'n Bibber like this before.
Never heard him say things right out this way. He was letting himself go. His eyes were wide open, and his body
was shaking.

"Farming is doing different things in different times
and seasons. It ain't working just to get grub. It ain't earning wages. It ain't so many dollars a day and a roof over
your head. It's being out in the seasons and following
them the year around. Bedding down your stock when the

snow is flying at night. Making friends with your cows. Smelling the hay when the air is full of frost. Tending a baby calf and teaching him to drink with your fingers in the gruel. Farming is smelling the new grass when it comes. It's planting and hoeing, and pitching hay till the sweat runs down your back. Seining up some smelts, maybe. Hustling to get things in ahead of the snow. Carrying the apples down cellar. Tasting cider made from your own apples. Cutting your own wood.

"You can't do farming the right way just with a lot of big machines. You've got to get down in the dirt. You don't work by the day. You don't work by the piece. You may have to put in fourteen hours on a hayfield or stay up all night when a cow's calving. Work from sunup to sundown. Make your day long as a day of summer. A small farm is a real farm. Where a man does all kinds of things for himself. Things that go right with the seasons. With his hands and his hind legs. Things for himself.

"Kennebec farming is the real kind. Our farms ain't big enough to get away from a man. They ain't big enough to make money on. You couldn't run a tractor on most of 'em if you tried. You'd knock the stuffing out of it. But we do a good job of farming on them just the same. We keep busy. We have more work than you can shake a stick at. And we don't keep an eye on no clock. We work for ourselves. We are our own boss. We don't take no orders from nobody.

"It's just the same with fishing. We own our boats and our nets. Nobody is going to tell us what to do except the wind and the tide. We don't get rich, but what we get is ours. We ain't working by the day. It's the right way for a man to live. Independent. That's the Kennebec way.

"They say it's the old-fashioned way. Maybe. But your Uncle Dudley notices that things ain't so hunky-dory with all them things the big efficiency experts has been running for the past fifty years. The wholesale business in raising grub and making money's sort of broken down. Gone to pot. And all this modern machinery's done for you and me is make a pair of pants so shoddy we can't straddle in 'em. Make paint that don't last two years. Tools that break when we put a strain on 'em. Maybe a little old-fashioned handiwork might be a good thing again. Things not made for the sake of money but for the sake of pride. Honesty. Maybe a lot of this machinery is what ails the world.

"And here we have all the smart alphabet-soup men from Washington down here doing their damnedest to make us Kennebec folks over. Make us measure work by the day and dollars we earn. 'Eight hours work, eight hours play, eight hours sleep, and eight dollars a day!' Four o'clock, time to knock off! Leave the last forkful of hay right in the air! Let the other six loads stay out overnight. Or charge yourself double wages if you get it in. Ain't that the hell of an idea?

"Them smart fellers will spoil you and me if they get a chance. They'll make eyeservants of us all. Work just when the boss has his eye on us. They'll teach our sons to work for five dollars a day and five hours. Not for the sake of feeling good because you're working. They'll tax our farms to make us pay the five dollars wages for the five-hour day. They'll make us pay the cost of ruining our children. And our sons will get city ideas and first chance they get, off they'll go to the city and stay there. Then where'll our farms be? Gone up the spout like so many of them round here. Lying idle. Full of hawkweed and hawks. Good pasture land taken back by the junipers. That ain't right. Something's wrong when small farms go under. Something's wrong with the U.S.A. Something damned rotten!"

Cap'n Bibber threw another spruce stick into the stove so hard the sparks showered up to the ceiling. He was a different man from the one I'd known for so many years. He had a glow on him, and it wasn't just the heat from the stove.

"And I can tell you another thing that's the matter. 'Tain't just the machinery and making hired men of us. People all over these United States has got the he's and she's all mixed up. You can't tell a he-one from a she-one among them summer folks here. Women have stole up on the men and got the pants away from them. Men don't wear mustaches much now, and that's too bad, for that's the last thing you could tell a lot of them was men by. We

need he-ones. Bad. Men who can stay by their lonesomes
and do the work men was made to do. Like the Kennebec
men.

"Honest, when I get to thinking about what we're
coming to, I lie awake nights. Men are getting scared
of living their lives now. Men are getting scared of being
alone. They want crowds around. They're scared of lonesomeness.

"My father brought his family up all by themselves out
on Long Island. We didn't see no other families for
months at a time. But we got along. We had a good time.
We young ones liked to go after the cows by ourselves and
never say a word to anybody, never see anybody for hours.
It was kind of sad, sometimes, after my father got lost in
the big blow of '88. Him and his schooner. Not ten miles
from home. I remember I'd go down and sit and think
of him for hours on the end of the island in the fog, and
listen to Seguin booming all by its lonesome, and the long
swells rolling in on the shore. It was powerful lonesome.

"But lonesomeness is what men need. A man needs to
be sad to be a well man. Along with other things. The
trouble is when it's all a man has. We've had our share of
trouble here along the Kennebec. We know what trouble
is."

Cap'n Bibber's voice was getting tired. He was speaking lower. He hardly moved the rocker. The shaving of a
moon had been gone for a long time from the window.
But the peepers were still there. I could hear them plainer
than ever. There seemed to be thousands now.

"It's a mighty sad thing to see women growing old un-
married. There are lots of them around here. Fussy about
their eating. Living in locked-up houses. And people who
was up in the world and had ships once, come down in life
and living on nothing but pride. Old men who had everything once, living in the kitchen, with their other rooms
closed up, and trying to keep warm over the kitchen stove.

"There's many's the fine old house round here I've
seen go downhill once the owner went out feet first
through his door, not caring any more about anything. No
children to keep the panes from falling out of the sashes.

And the swallows coming in through the broken glass, and nesting on the mantels. It's bad to have a fine house go to pieces like that. It makes a man feel sorry. Houses without living in them, going to pieces fast. The old people who built lots of the houses round here must be turning in their graves. The rain and wind coming into the rooms where their children was born, and nobody around to care. By and by, there's nothing but a cellar. And nobody knows who ever lived there. Like that cellar place in my west pasture. That's the way a man dies twice, and all over, and for good.

"The old hulls rotting away at the pier at Wiscasset. I don't hanker to look at them when I'm down there. They was full of good men once, and now they are rotten wood and Toledo worms. They carried goods once, and now they're empty. Fine schooners, dead as the captains that sailed them, up in the graveyard.

"There's sad things enough on the Kennebec. Only we ain't the kind to talk about them much. We don't keep rolling our shirts up to show where we are hard hit. 'Tain't the Kennebec way."

The lamp had burned low. The firelight came out through the grate in the stove and danced on the ceiling. The fire was getting low, too. The dim color of it touched the captain's gray hair and made hollows of his cheeks and eyes.

"The worst thing of all is the farms growing up to trees. The birches and maples coming over the stone walls. The hemlocks and frost tipping over the stones. The forest comes back and takes back the fields men sweat blood to clear. Little pines coming up through the hay, and pretty soon there's no hay there. The woods close in round the orchard. The chipmunks and partridges gather the apples. There's no boy around to keep them away. Not a sign of anybody at the windows of the house. It ain't a farm any more, just a forest. And that's where people lived once and raised good corn and big families.

"There's more wild land along the Kennebec Valley today then there was hundred years ago.

"It makes a man lonesome."

Cap'n Bibber didn't have anything more to say. He had stopped rocking for good. He sat there without moving. After a while he took his feet out of the oven and closed the door. He gazed at the last glow of the fire. The faint light made him seem suddenly thin in the face. Like an old, old man.

There was a quick step on the stoop and the door banged open, enough to jar the whole house.

"Take it easy, Bill!" Cap'n Bibber growled. "Do you want to have the door off the hinges?"

"Oh, Dad!" said Bill. "She's going to marry me next month!"

"Good work," said Cap'n Cy. "Good work, son!"

# 27 The River of the Future

Greed has fouled the Kennebec. The business that does not last, that produces the cheap things that crumble away in the using, has poisoned the great river that sweeps from Moosehead to the sea. Shortsighted men have stripped the finest plumes of the ancient pines from the hills. The beaver and the sturgeon have joined the red men. The tides of silver that used to sweep in with the spring—the shad and herring—are gone for the time. The trout have retreated to the cleaner, smaller streams. The ships and steamboats that once carried life out and over the oldest highway of man are gone. A whole day may go past and no living human sign pass Fort Popham. The lighthouses turn their anxious eyes around and around and waste their wakefulness on an empty river and ocean.

But the promise of life is still there. The cleanness of snows and rains and vast crystals of lakes are still in the hills, ready to restore the river. The shad swim still, all the way up from Florida, eager to enter the Kennebec whenever men say the word. The old nets that hang in the open chambers may someday be mended and spread out among the June daisies with flakes of silver fish scales starring them. The herring turn their sharp noses each year toward Kennebec's mouth. They would be glad to fill Merrymeeting Bay with treasure once more. After the great floods of March 1936 had swept some of the riverbed clean, salmon and bass and alewives were seen leaping the falls at Brunswick. But in a few weeks, purple dyes were being vomited into the river and the leaping silver fish were gone.

There are three great nourishers of life asleep in Maine, along the Kennebec. Let men say the word and they will shake off their sleep and fill this windy and sunny northeast corner of America full of a life more abundant than ever was here in the past. Fisheries, forests, and merchant marine, these three can again make Maine a leader of the nation. Then she will no longer need to take in summer boarders. Her children will not have to go elsewhere to make a living and get up in the world, as many of them have had to do recently; there will be plenty of work for them at home. These three resources, wisely husbanded, will furnish a perpetual wealth in contented and busy citizens; and once more Maine can live up to the motto on her escutcheon, *Dirigo*, "I lead."

Sailboats have appeared of late and whitened the mouth of the Kennebec. These are the craft of vacationing summer people. But their number can be multiplied a hundredfold in a few summers, with natives at their tillers. The fishermen can come back and make Kennebec the feeder of Europe again, as it was two hundred years ago when Dr. Noyes, one of the Kennebec proprietors, had his fleet fishing for sturgeon to garnish the London tables and nourish the bright wits of Addison and Steele and Pope. Stop the pollution by the mills and the cities, replenish the river from the hatcheries and lakes, and "Kennebec salmon" need no longer be only a name on every hotel menu, and a myth, but can return to the nation's table in its own person to rebuke the present forgers and charlatans from other waters.

The alewives can fill Merrymeeting Bay again, and smokehouses become as common as woodsheds. Merrymeeting is large enough to mint a nation's wealth in the silver currency of herring and shad.

As to timber, Maine can become a land richer in forests than Sweden, with a farmed forestry, where there is no waste, where trees are cared for like children for the children of tomorrow. Maine's lumber crop is still almost as great in bulk as it was in the nineteenth century, though now a traffic in small stuff. The fertility of Maine's forests is one of the amazing miracles of our time. It has stood up under two hundred years of constant shortsightedness. The wholesale destruction of thousands of square miles of evergreens and the leavings of slashing to turn into tinder and burn up the new growth and even the soil below it in forest fires—that has been the history of man's folly the past hundred years. And yet without new planting, without protection, the pines and spruces have come trooping bravely back, have created new soil and new moisture and new forests. And this evergreen empire could be made tenfold greater if men would assist the tough resourcefulness of a soil that is bound to bring forth forests to house the children of the future.

America was once the greatest nation in the world in her merchant marine, and Maine the leader in it. She could be so again. With the timber fit for the wooden parts of ships growing taller and clearer of knots, and with her sons increasing in numbers and training themselves on the hundreds of her bays from boyhood, there would be the men to man an American merchant marine larger than that of the 1840s and '50s. Maine is the natural cradle for a commonwealth of seafaring man, better than Scotland and better than Sweden. With the lumber trade growing and the fisheries flourishing, there would be cargoes here for the whole world. Maine has the harbors, scores of them far up the deep bays and rivers, with natural breakwaters and natural defenses. The state has more good harbors than any country in the world I know. Harbors and the cargoes and men promised that could fill them.

These makers of life once flourished on the Kennebec. They could do so again.

The Kennebec has one kind of wealth, too, that has never been exhausted. It is a wealth that means much to a nation. Maybe it is the greatest of all. Greece found it so. A culture needs it at its roots if it is a culture that is going to endure. The Kennebec's wealth, which no carelessness of men could ever destroy, is beauty. The river is one of the earth's loveliest. That beauty has clung on in the woods of white pines that nothing could stamp out, not man's greed nor fires in the slashing left by portable sawmills. Woods that are harps in the winds. Blue herons sweep the bays in hundreds in effortless flight, their necks curved back like kings'. The woodcock and the partridge walk with bright eyes in the meadow next to the cornfield. Beauty has stayed on in the old farmhouses under the seraphs of elms whose wings touch over the ridgepole. In deep and sunny valleys, white houses and white barns hold lives whose centers are still fixed in cradles and nests full of warm new eggs and cider in straw-covered demijohns. Houses sweetened by many generations of living, where the present master of the houses goes up to love and sleep on stairs hollowed out by the feet of his grandfather and great-grandfather. The names on the mailboxes are the same as those on the stones in the small graveyard at the loveliest corner of the farm, where the grapes grow up the stone wall. The highways on both sides of the river run through such patterns of peace, high farms ripping down to the blue water under a sky filled with swallows, checkerboards of small gardens where potatoes and corn ears are like members of a family, closed in by stone walls laid up by boys on their way to be tall men. Small churches and small schoolhouses along the highroad, almost empty now, but the children who may fill them full with children and men and women again are carrying cool drinks to the mowers, are warming their cut-me-downs from their fathers' old trousers as they drive home the cows with the evening sound of bells. Little tucked-away towns, Dresden and Richmond and Bowdoinham, drowsy since the last ship sailed from their wharves, left on one side by the new roads of concrete and macadam that have drained life away from the river. Drowsy but with life still warm in them, ready to wake and work. Later Edwin Arlington Robinsons may be walking the dusty streets of those towns this minute, barefooted and with faces too bright to believe, on their way to meet Arthur and Tristram as contemporaries and equals in the village schools. Coals have come down to us hot from the fires that once made these riverbanks roar with life, when Maine farmers went around the Horn and Good Hope for their honeymoons and came home with their arms to the elbows in the spices of Java and China tea. These coals can spring up in new fires. Where a dozen good men drive their spans of oxen now a hundred can lay open the soil. There is room for them there, in houses built for the big families of long ago, in the fields too large for a lonely plowman.

My house on Merrymeeting Bay, where I write these lines, is only one among many places waiting to flower again by the river that runs through the heart of Maine. A fireplace wide enough to take a family of twelve into its warm arms, a fireplace in every room, and cranes and S-hooks to hold kettles for porridge in them all. That is the kind of place a home ought to be. Bedrooms above, paneled in pine cut on the farm, golden brown and velvety with the sunshine and use of many years. Door latches made by hand and worn away by the hands of many people who sprang from the loins of the maker. Eye-hooks to hold the rug frames in the kitchen ceiling, and all the delicate wooden vitals of a hand loom stowed in the attic, waiting to be set up again and minister to a new family, each small reed and bobbin made by hand. A shad net hangs there too, high up so the mice cannot gnaw it, among the ax-hewn rafters that are pegged with wooden pins instead of nails. There are pantries with half doors and a sloping out-side cellar door waiting to lift up and let life in and out again. The walls of this house of mine are not merely pan-eled wood and plaster, they are the rhythms of life and love that went on inside them, they are the stuff of loyalties and fealties that could not be buried under six feet of cold earth in the little graveyard back of the grape arbor. The walls are alive and they call out to the life in me and my children.

Wherever I sit, I can look through small panes with flat eighteenth-century sashes and see old friends of the family. Trees come up close to my house to look in on the living going on here. Every north window frames a pasture pine growing from the crumbling stone wall. Even on a wind-less day, those vast old trees whisper together back and forth, one waiting till the other has finished, passing on mysterious messages that lie at the roots of beauty and music. There are other sagas of early America in the worn grindstone and farming implements in the barn. I come on

old poems in horse sleds left out among the elderberry
bushes, poems lean and touch my window in the loaded
bough of a crab apple tree. The white everlasting roses
crowd up to my pasture bars, frost-flowers climb up the
ledges to the pines that are centuries old. The two barns
have grown into the rolling fields around them and taken
their color. A brook comes down to join the Kennebec
through a valley deep as a dream. A family roadway runs
down through pine needles and white clover to my own
harbor on Merrymeeting. It was a road to life once and it
is a road to life again, now that my sons run on it. It points
them the way to fishing and hunting as it pointed it two
hundred years ago for other small boys who lived before
mine in my house, as it probably showed the way to naked
brown Abenaki boys a thousand years before their time.

But there are many houses like mine that have no small
boys in them. I have reclaimed only one. The others call
out for men to come and move in, mend their roofs and
put back the panes, set up the stones in their stone walls,
and repair the pasture bars. There are abandoned farms
where there is everything worth living for. Beauty of trees
and hills and waters, valleys and high ledges, places for
cows and sheep. All that is needed is the chance for men to
have the fish or the ships or the forests, to supplement the
little gardens and hayfields, and to give the opportunity to
multiply their kind.

The harvest of clean air and the sharp Maine light is
being garnered by those who know how to collect the
treasure that lasts. The summer folks gather the cleanness
and beauty in, along with the few natives. But there ought
to be more native people to join them.

I have a friend, an artist, who has staked his claim to
the very mouth of my river. He has bought himself a
whole cape on Long Island, Gilbert Head, a granite cliff
that divides the mighty current and looks out over Popham
and Pond to Seguin's lighthouse and the whole Atlantic.
He has a vast white house and a forest of Maine spruces
behind to back it up against the rush of the southeast
gales. Gannets brush his eaves as they sweep past forever.
Sea gulls snow the black runes of fierce and tormented

water where the Kennebec's might meets the incoming tide. It is bold water below his doorstep. His cliff goes down more than a hundred feet into the abyss where the two strengths grapple through all time: the cod swims under his windows. He looks out on every kind of beauty that wind and sky and river and ocean, beach and forest and rock can make. He lives in the midst of hymns, which are the voice of very ancient laws. Storms are his nearest neighbors and the fogs come upon him like armies of friends. The daily drama of tides and winds and the rushing out of a great river is played at his front door. And my friend is putting this epic of light and shadow, the powerful loveliness he sees every moment of his day, into his pictures. And his pictures will go out into a world wider than that which was cooled by Kennebec's ice in the old days, and they will keep the record of this place of crystal and azure.

He has caught the uniqueness of Maine, its sea and evergreens and the dust of the rainbows that drench Maine houses and Maine people with their radiance and get into the very living here.

Other people have begun to discover the wealth that is Maine. Native novelists and poets are beginning to tell America about the brightness of the place and the people, about tough human beings with the sparkle of wit in them, and the glint of granite. These authors of the new Maine school of writing are one of the most promising features of today's literary landscape. They are one of the sturdiest crops, surely, that Maine has. They are not singing elegies, either. They are telling the world about an everlasting vigor that some people had got to thinking was antique. Just when the rest of the country thought that the New England culture was finished and Puritanism safely in the museum, these new poets of the people have put up their heads and have begun to tell, as shrilly as peepers in April, that the best in New England character is still here among us: the stern code of the level head and the stout heart. They are telling an America threatened with standardization that rugged individualists still live in this clear corner of the land. Men and women who stand the test of New

England winters and come out into the summers smiling: who can weather adversity and grow by it. If you would catch an echo of the everlasting law nature decreed for Maine, read Gladys Hasty Carroll, who writes of people who fit into the rhythm of the seasons and are the salt of the earth, read Mary Ellen Chase and Wilbert Snow. Folks such as these writers put into their books are living now around the Kennebec.

From the days when the lean Abenaki hunted these forests and waters, through the periods when the settlers came from Britain, Ireland, Europe, and into the time of the blended stocks that are the present inhabitants, the Kennebec folk have been a tough, bright, and smart people. Their fiber has not weakened during depressions, because they are able to grip rock and live as lichens do. Clean water is their primal need. Give them that to refresh their energies and the Kennebec River again will flow over the world.

# Acknowledgement

There are a lot of people I ought to thank for helping me with this book. But if I listed them all, I should have to rewrite a good deal of my life's story. Friends and relations who helped raise me or grew up with me had a hand in this undertaking by being the Maine kind of people they were. I thank them all now with my book's contents. In particular, I make my acknowledgments to my brother, Frank L. Coffin, who is one of the fast vanishing breed of oral storytellers.

My friends Ted and Eleanor Emery took me to one of the finest Kennebec houses, overlooking the spot where Arnold's bateaux were built, and they turned me loose in the best private collection of historical material about Maine. The Emerys also supplied me with lore from their own section of the Kennebec.

I wish to acknowledge my indebtedness to the Collections of the Maine Historical Society. Any wayfarer into Maine's past must be proud of this organization. I wish to thank also the librarians at the Maine State Library in Augusta, for giving me the key to the place and trusting in me, on one occasion, to lock up for them. The people in the Bowdoin College Library have been patient with me no end. I do not know how many other librarians I ought to thank, but a great many, I am sure, in different towns.

Many individuals have been generous in assisting me, too. In particular, I make grateful mention of Mr. Louis Burton Woodward of Gorham, Miss Lillian Russell of Warren, Mr. Harold Pulsifer of Brunswick, my wife, of course, as always, and my old friend and colleague, Wilmot B. Mitchell.

Among the town histories I have read, there are two recent ones that I think are of special distinction: Charles E. Allen's *History of Dresden* and Henry W. Owen's *History of Bath*.

Robert P. Tristram Coffin
North Woolwich
Merrymeeting Bay, Maine
March, 1937

# Index